QUICK AND EASY
PASTA SAUCES

QUICK AND EASY PASTA SAUCES

By
Carolyn Humphries

foulsham

LONDON · NEW YORK · TORONTO · SYDNEY

foulsham

The Publishing House, Bennetts Close,
Cippenham, Berkshire, SL1 5AP, England.

ISBN 0-572-02272-7

Printed in Great Britain by
Cox & Wyman Ltd, Reading, Berkshire.

CONTENTS

INTRODUCTION

Pasta isn't a modern convenience food – it has been eaten all over the world for centuries. Even the Ancient Egyptians tucked in to bowls of noodles. But it has to be one of the most versatile and nutritious staple foods today. There are so many varieties to choose from, all of which are simple and quick to cook. They can then be bathed in any number of sauces to turn them into meals fit for every occasion.

This book is crammed full of taste-tingling ideas with flavours from many different lands. You will be able to create authentic classic specialities and many exciting new dishes quickly and easily. There are tips on the different types of pasta too and how to cook them. There's even a very simple recipe for making your own. So to pasta lovers everywhere, this is for you.

PASTA FACT FILE

Varieties
There are over six hundred different pasta shapes made in Italy alone. They are made in a variety of colours and flavours – the standard pale, creamy durum wheat; the more golden, egg pasta; the popular green, spinach; the rustic wholewheat; the glorious orangey, sun-dried tomato; the black, mushroom or the speckled olive-flavoured to name but a few. Then there are the exciting varieties of noodles from the Far East and the flat noodles of German-speaking countries too. It is impossible to list every one in this little book, but here are some of the main ones you are likely to use. Most varieties are available fresh or dried.

Strands
Long threads of pasta in different thicknesses.

Spaghetti: probably the best known of all pastas, it is long, thin and straight.

Capelli d'angelo or Capellini: 'angel hair', the thinnest of all.

Fusilli: 'fuses'- thick spaghetti.

Spaghettini: 'little spaghetti'.

Vermicelli: 'little worms'.

Tubes
There are many shapes and sizes of tubes. These are some of the most common.

Bucatini: long macaroni, like spaghetti but thicker with a hole in the middle.

Cannelloni: large fat tubes, served stuffed.

Ditali: short-cut macaroni, narrow tubes.

Elbow macaroni: short, curved, narrow tubes.

Penne: quill-shaped tubes.

Rigatoni: ribbed tubes.

Zite: wide macaroni cut in short lengths.

Shapes
There is a superb variety of shapes to choose from, including the following types.

Conchiglie: conch-shaped shells.

Farfalle: butterflies.

Lumachi: snail-shaped shells.

Maltagliate: 'badly cut' pasta. Make from fresh pasta (see page 11).

Maruzze: shells of varying sizes.

Rotelli or twistetti: spirals.

Ruote: wheels.

Ribbon Noodles
These are made from flat pasta cut into varying widths, sometimes kept flat, sometimes with a rippled edge.

Fettuccine: flat ribbons about 5 mm/^{1}/$_4$ in wide.

Fettuccelli: narrow fettuccine.

Fettucci: as above, but about 1 cm/^{1}/$_2$ in wide.

Linguini: very narrow ribbons, like flattened spaghetti.

Mafalde: wide ribbons with a rippled edge.

Pappardelle: wide ribbons about 2 cm/^{3}/$_4$ in wide.

Tagliarini: narrow tagliatelle (see below).

Tagliatelle: similar to fettuccine.

Stuffed Shapes

Cheese, spinach, mushroom and meat stuffings are all popular.

Agnolotti: small, filled half-moons.

Cappelletti: little, filled hat shapes.

Ravioli: stuffed cushions.

Tortellini: small crescent shapes joined into rings.

Chinese Noodles

Quicker to cook than Italian pasta and some, like cellophane noodles, need to be soaked before cooking.

Egg noodles: wiggly strands, sold in square-shaped nests.

Wheat noodles: sold in square-shaped nests or as long spaghetti-like strands.

Rice noodles or sticks: white strands.

Rice vermicelli: very thin white threads.

Arrowroot vermicelli: sold in pure white bundles.

Cellophane or pea starch noodles: transparent thin strands.

Chow mein noodles: yellow fried noodles.

Japanese Noodles

If you cannot find the following, substitute Chinese noodles instead.

Harusame: like cellophane noodles.

Soba: thin brownish noodles made from buckwheat flour.

Somen: fine white noodles, like vermicelli.

Udon: more filling wheat flour noodles.

QUICK AND EASY FRESH PASTA

You can mix the dough by hand, working the flour into the eggs then kneading until smooth, but it takes longer!

Serves 4	Metric	Imperial	American
Eggs	*3*	*3*	*3*
Strong (bread) flour	*275 g*	*10 oz*	*2¹/₂ cups*
Flour for dusting			
Salt			
Olive oil	*15 ml*	*1 tbsp*	*1 tbsp*

1. Break the eggs into a food processor and run the machine for 30 seconds.

2. Add the flour and blend for a further 30 seconds or until mixture forms a soft but not sticky dough.

3. Turn out onto a floured board and knead until the dough is smooth and elastic, adding a little more flour if getting sticky.

4. Wrap in a polythene bag and leave on the side for 30 minutes to rest.

5. On a large floured surface roll out and stretch the dough, rolling away from you and giving it a quarter turn every so often until it is thin enough to almost see through and hanging over the edge of the work surface. For shapes, cut now (see below); for tagliatelle, cover with a cloth and leave for 15 minutes before cutting.

To Shape

Cannelloni/Lasagne: Cut the rolled dough into oblongs 10 × 13 cm/4 × 5 in. Boil in lightly salted water for 1 minute then place in a bowl of cold water with 5 ml/1 tsp oil added. Drain on a damp cloth.

Farfalle: Cut the rolled dough into 5 cm/2 in squares with a fluted pastry wheel. Pinch the squares together diagonally across the middle to form butterflies or bows.

Maltagliate: This literally means 'badly cut'. Simply cut the rolled dough into small triangles about the size of a thumb nail. Used mainly in soups.

Pappardelle: Cut the rolled dough with a plain or fluted cutter into strips 2 cm/^{3}/$_4$ in wide.

Ravioli: Cut dough in half and roll out each half to a similar sized square or rectangle. Put 5 ml/1 tsp of chosen filling at regular intervals in rows across one sheet of dough. Brush all round with water. Lay second sheet on top and press down gently between each pile of filling. Use a fluted pastry wheel to cut between filling down the length and then across the width to form little cushions of filled pasta.

Tagliatelle: Roll up the rested sheet of pasta like a Swiss (jelly) roll. Cut into slices about 5mm/^{1}/$_4$ in thick. Unroll and drape over a clean cloth on the back of a chair (or a clothes–horse) while you cut the rest.

Note: If you are a pasta fanatic, you could buy a pasta machine to roll and cut the dough into professional-looking shapes. The best ones, in my opinion, are chrome-plated with stainless steel rollers.

To Cook
Allow 100 g/4 oz/1 cup pasta per person

1. Bring a large pan of lightly salted water to the boil.

2. Add 15 ml/1 tbsp olive oil or a knob of butter and the pasta and cook for about 4 minutes until almost tender but not soggy (al dente). Drain and use as required.

To Cook Dried Pasta

Follow packet directions, allowing 50-100 g/2-4 oz/ $1/2$-1 cup of pasta per person (according to appetites). Add oil or butter as above to prevent the water boiling over.

To Microwave (in a 650 watt oven)

Dried Pasta: For 4 people, put 225 g/8 oz/2 cups pasta (break spaghetti-types into thirds for even cooking), into a large microwave safe bowl. Add 900 ml/$1^1/2$ pts/$3^3/4$ cups boiling water, 5 ml/1 tsp salt and 10 ml/2 tsp olive oil. Cook uncovered for 12-15 minutes on full power, stirring gently 4 times. Cover and leave to stand for 6-8 minutes until pasta swells and absorbs most of the water. Drain and use as required.

Note: Reduce cooking time slightly for a higher output oven, increase it for a lower one.

Fresh pasta: For 4 people, cook as above but use only 600 ml/1 pt/$2^1/2$ cups boiling water. Cook for half the time and leave to stand for 5 minutes.

NOTES ON THE RECIPES

- When following a recipe use EITHER Metric, Imperial or American measures, never mix them up.

- All spoon measures are level.

- All eggs are size 3 unless otherwise stated.

- Always wash, dry and peel, if necessary, fresh produce before use.

- Fresh herbs are used unless dried are specified in the recipe.

- All preparation and cooking times are approximate and should be used as a guide only. Remember to allow for the cooking time of the pasta (cook it at the same time as making the sauce).

- Every recipe suggests a type of pasta with which to serve the sauce, but any pasta can be served with any sauce – the choice is yours.

- Many of the pasta sauces do not contain meat or fish so are suitable for vegetarians. But make sure the cheese you use is also suitable. In supermarkets these are usually clearly marked.

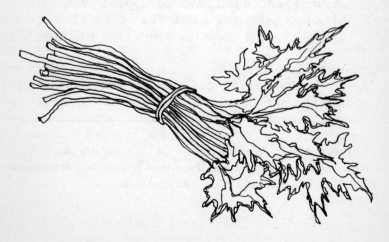

ACCOMPANIMENTS

The lovely thing about pasta is it needs very little accompaniment. However, as the sauces can be quite rich, a simple salad and/or some warm crusty bread will round off the meal to perfection.

Simple Salads

- Crisp Leaf Salad: Either buy a bag of ready-prepared mixed leaves from your supermarket (expensive but useful if you're short of time) or make your own selection from the numerous varieties available. Tear rather than chop and place in a bowl. Dress with a simple vinaigrette: 3 parts olive oil to 1 part wine vinegar. Season with salt, pepper and a pinch of caster (superfine) sugar.

- Tomato and Onion Salad: Slice firm, ripe tomatoes and place in a shallow dish. Top with thinly sliced onion rings and dress with vinaigrette (see above). Sprinkle with chopped parsley or a few torn basil leaves and leave to stand for 30 minutes to allow the flavours to develop.

- Mixed Green Salad: Mix any type of green salad leaves in a bowl. Add sliced cucumber, green (bell) pepper, cut into thin strips or rings, a few chopped spring onions (scallions) and sliced avocado, dipped in lemon juice. Add a little Dijon mustard to the vinaigrette (see above) and sprinkle the whole thing with mustard cress.

Beautiful breads

A warm ordinary crusty loaf is delicious but you could try something a little more adventurous. The best speciality breads to go with pasta are either Ciabatta (plain or flavoured with olives, mushrooms, sun-dried tomatoes, herbs, garlic or walnuts) or French bread either plain or try one of the ready-to-bake flavoured butter baguettes like garlic, herb, cheese, or cheese and bacon.

MEAT & POULTRY SAUCES

All the following recipes make memorable main courses but can be served in smaller portions as starters if you prefer.

EVERYDAY BOLOGNESE

This is a family favourite, but not an authentic Italian sauce. See page 18 for Ragu alla Bolognese

Serves 4	Metric	Imperial	American
Minced (ground) beef or lamb	*350 g*	*12 oz*	*3 cups*
Onion, chopped	*1*	*1*	*1*
Garlic clove, crushed	*1*	*1*	*1*
Can chopped tomatoes	*400 g*	*14 oz*	*1 large can*
Tomato purée (paste)	*15 ml*	*1 tbsp*	*1 tbsp*
Salt and freshly ground black pepper			
Dried oregano	*5 ml*	*1 tsp*	*1 tsp*
Pinch of caster (superfine) sugar			
To serve			
Freshly grated Parmesan cheese			

1. Put the meat, onion and garlic in a saucepan. Cook stirring until the meat is browned and in grains.

2. Add the remaining ingredients. Stir well. Bring to the boil, reduce heat, half-cover and simmer gently for 15-20 minutes until a rich sauce has formed. Stir gently from time to time.

Serving suggestions
Spoon over cooked spaghetti or other long pasta or add to cooked pasta shapes and toss well. Alternatively use to stuff cannelloni. Serve with grated Parmesan cheese sprinkled over.

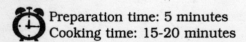
Preparation time: 5 minutes
Cooking time: 15-20 minutes

FOR A SIMPLE LASAGNE

Put a spoonful of the meat mixture in the base of a fairly shallow ovenproof dish. Top with strips of no-need-to-precook lasagne. Add half the remaining sauce, more lasagne, the rest of the sauce then a final layer of lasagne. Top with Basic Cheese Sauce (see page 127) and bake at 190°C/375°F/gas mark 5 for 35 minutes until cooked through and golden brown. Or microwave for about 15 minutes or until the lasagne feels tender when a knife is inserted down through the centre. Then place under a hot grill (broiler) to brown top.

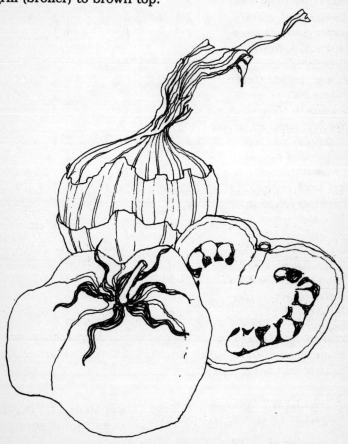

Ragu alla Bolognese

Italian housewives would simmer this sauce for several hours, moistening with a little more wine as necessary. Do try doing so yourself if you have the time. For an even better flavour, leave it to stand overnight then reheat it the following day. Use as for Everyday Bolognese.

Serves 6	Metric	Imperial	American
Olive oil	45 ml	3 tbsp	3 tbsp
Onion, finely chopped	1	1	1
Garlic cloves, crushed	2	2	2
Carrot, finely chopped	1	1	1
Celery stick, finely chopped	1	1	1
Minced (ground) beef	450 g	l lb	4 cups
Streaky bacon rashers (slices), chopped	3	3	3
Ripe beef tomatoes, skinned, seeded and chopped	3	3	3
OR chopped canned tomatoes	400 g	14 oz	1 large can
Beef stock	150 ml	$^1/_4$ pt	$^2/_3$ cup
Wineglass red wine	1	1	1
Thick slice lemon	1	1	1
Bay leaf	1	1	1
Salt and freshly ground black pepper			
Tomato purée (paste)	15 ml	1 tbsp	1 tbsp
Double (heavy) cream (optional)	30 ml	2 tbsp	2 tbsp
To serve			
Freshly grated Parmesan cheese			

1.   Heat the olive oil in a large saucepan and fry (sauté) the onion, garlic, carrot and celery for 3 minutes until softened but not browned.

2. Add the beef and bacon and fry, stirring until browned and the grains of meat are separate.

3. Add the tomatoes, stock, wine, the thick slice of lemon and the bay leaf. Season with salt and pepper and bring to the boil, stirring.

4. Reduce the heat and simmer gently, uncovered until the sauce is well reduced and thick, about 30 minutes (or cook in a slo-cooker for 5-6 hours).

5. Discard the lemon slice and bay leaf. Taste and re-season if necessary. Stir in the cream, if using. Serve as for Everyday Bolognese with grated Parmesan cheese sprinkled over.

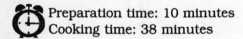
Preparation time: 10 minutes
Cooking time: 38 minutes

RICH STEAK SAUCE

This is a quick version of a sauce my gran used to call 'Bolognese' when I was a child. It's nothing like the Italian sauce, but it is truly delicious. She would prepare it in a flameproof casserole then cook it in a slow oven (160°C/325°F/gas mark 3) for about 3 hours (which is worth doing if you have the time).

Serves 4-6	Metric	Imperial	American
Onions, finely chopped	*2*	*2*	*2*
Dripping or lard (shortening)	*25 g*	*1 oz*	*2 tbsp*
Lean top rump steak, minced (ground)	*450 g*	*1 lb*	*4 cups*
Beef stock	*450 ml*	*³/4 pt*	*2 cups*
A little gravy salt or browning			
Salt and freshly ground black pepper to taste			
Plain (all-purpose) flour	*25 g*	*1 oz*	*¹/4 cup*
To garnish			
Warmed passata (sieved tomatoes) or ketchup (catsup)			
Chopped parsley			

1. Fry (sauté) the onion in the dripping until softened and lightly golden.

2. Add the steak and fry stirring until browned and the grains are separate.

3. Add the stock and a little gravy salt or browning. Half cover and simmer gently for 30-40 minutes until really tender (or cook in a pressure cooker for 20 minutes or a slo-cooker for up to 6 hours).

4. Blend the flour with a little water until smooth. Stir into the meat and bring to the boil. Simmer, stirring for 2 minutes. Season to taste with salt and pepper.

Serving suggestion

Spoon over a pile of cooked spaghetti, drizzle with a little warmed passata (sieved tomatoes) or ketchup (catsup) and sprinkle with chopped parsley.

 Preparation time: 5 minutes
Cooking time: 45 minutes

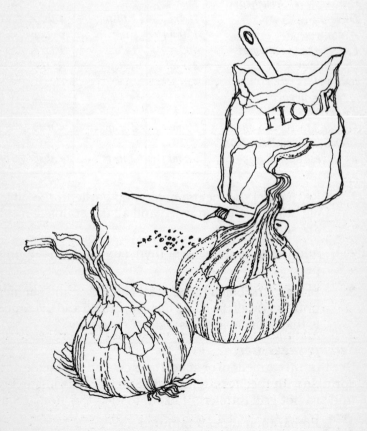

MOZZARELLA-TOPPED VEAL AND PORK SAUCE

If you don't like veal then use all pork in this simple ragu.

Serves 4	Metric	Imperial	American
Minced (ground) veal	175 g	6 oz	1¹/₂ cups
Minced (ground) pork	175 g	6 oz	1¹/₂ cups
Onion, finely chopped	1	1	1
Garlic cloves, crushed	2	2	2
Olive oil	15 ml	1 tbsp	1 tbsp
White wine	150 ml	¹/₄ pt	²/₃ cup
Can chopped tomatoes	400 g	14 oz	1 large can
Dried thyme	2.5 ml	¹/₂ tsp	¹/₂ tsp
Salt and freshly ground black pepper			
To serve			
Grated Mozzarella cheese	60 ml	4 tbsp	4 tbsp
Freshly grated Parmesan cheese	30 ml	2 tbsp	2 tbsp

1. Fry (sauté) the meats, onion and garlic in the olive oil, stirring until browned and all the grains of meat are separate.

2. Add the wine, tomatoes, thyme and a little salt and pepper.

3. Bring to the boil, reduce heat, part-cover and simmer until nearly all the liquid has evaporated and the sauce is thick. Taste and re-season if necessary.

Serving suggestion
Use to stuff cannelloni or spoon over cooked tagliatelle and sprinkle with the Mozzarella and Parmesan. Flash quickly under a hot grill (broiler), if liked, to melt the Mozzarella.

 Preparation time: 5 minutes
Cooking time: 35 minutes

PARMA HAM AND MUSHROOM SAUCE

Any of the raw thin-sliced hams can be used in this recipe.

Serves 4	Metric	Imperial	American
Olive oil	30 ml	2 tbsp	2 tbsp
Button mushrooms, sliced	100 g	4 oz	2 cups
Yeast extract	5 ml	1 tsp	1 tsp
Parma ham, cut in thin strips	100 g	4 oz	1 cup
Butter	25 g	1 oz	2 tbsp
Crème fraîche	75 ml	5 tbsp	5 tbsp
Salt and freshly ground black pepper			
Grated nutmeg	1.5 ml	1/4 tsp	1/4 tsp
To serve			
Freshly grated Parmesan or Pecorino cheese			

1. Heat oil in a small saucepan and add the mushrooms. Cook gently for 2 minutes until softened.

2. Stir in the yeast extract, ham strips, and the butter in small flakes. Heat gently stirring until butter melts.

3. Stir in the crème fraîche, salt and pepper to taste and the nutmeg. Heat through for 2 minutes.

Serving suggestion
Add to any cooked ribbon pasta and toss well over a gentle heat before serving with grated Parmesan or Pecorino cheese.

 Preparation time: 5 minutes
Cooking time: 5 minutes

PIQUANT CHICKEN LIVER SAUCE

Don't serve grated cheese with this sauce, just a cool tomato and onion salad as an accompaniment.

Serves 4	Metric	Imperial	American
Onions, finely chopped	2	2	2
Butter	25 g	1 oz	2 tbsp
Olive oil	15 ml	1 tbsp	1 tbsp
Wineglass red vermouth	1	1	1
Chicken livers, trimmed and finely chopped	450 g	1 lb	4 cups
Chopped sage	5 ml	1 tsp	1 tsp
Salt and freshly ground black pepper			
To garnish			
Chopped parsley			

1. Fry (sauté) the onions in the butter and oil until soft but not brown.

2. Add the vermouth and simmer until reduced by half.

3. Add the chicken livers and sage and cook quickly until brown but not dry, about 2-3 minutes. Season to taste.

Serving suggestion

Add to cooked farfalle or other pasta of your choice, toss well and sprinkle with chopped parsley before serving.

Preparation time: 10 minutes
Cooking time: 7-8 minutes

KIDNEY AND MUSTARD SAUCE

For a change, try using a grainy mustard instead of Dijon.

Serves 4-6	Metric	Imperial	American
Lambs' kidneys	4	4	4
Butter	40 g	1½ oz	3 tbsp
Olive oil	15 ml	1 tbsp	1 tbsp
Brandy	30 ml	2 tbsp	2 tbsp
Dijon mustard	15 ml	1 tbsp	1 tbsp
Double (heavy) cream	60 ml	4 tbsp	4 tbsp
Salt and freshly ground black pepper			
Snipped chives	30 ml	2 tbsp	2 tbsp
To garnish			
Toasted buttered breadcrumbs			

1. Peel off any skin on the kidneys then cut in halves. Snip out the cores with scissors then snip the kidneys into small pieces.

2. Heat the butter and oil in a frying pan (skillet). Add the kidneys and cook stirring for 2-3 minutes until browned and tender. Do not overcook.

3. Add the brandy and ignite. When the flames die down add the mustard and cream and heat through, stirring until well blended. Season to taste and stir in the chives.

Serving suggestion
Spoon onto a bed of cooked tagliarini and sprinkle with toasted buttered breadcrumbs.

Preparation time: 10 minutes
Cooking time: 5 minutes

BEEF STROGANOFF SAUCE

This special occasion sauce is ideal for a dinner party and makes a little fillet steak go a long way.

Serves 4	Metric	Imperial	American
Fillet steak	225 g	8 oz	1/2 lb
Butter	50 g	2 oz	1/4 cup
Onions, thinly sliced	2	2	2
Button mushrooms, sliced	100 g	4 oz	2 cups
Salt and freshly ground black pepper			
Brandy	15 ml	1 tbsp	1 tbsp
Soured (dairy sour) cream	150 ml	1/4 pt	2/3 cup
To garnish			
Knob of butter			
Chopped parsley			

1. Cut the steak into thin strips about 2.5 cm/1 in long.

2. Heat half the butter in a large frying pan. Add the onions and fry (sauté) for 2-3 minutes until softened and lightly golden.

3. Add the mushrooms and continue cooking, stirring for 2-3 minutes until cooked through. Remove from the pan and reserve.

4. Heat the remaining butter and add the beef. Season well with salt and pepper and fry, stirring for about 3 minutes until just cooked through.

5. Add the brandy, ignite and shake pan until the flames subside.

6. Return the onions and mushrooms to the pan with any cooking juices. Stir in the cream and heat through.

Serving suggestion

Toss any cooked ribbon noodles in the butter. Spoon over the stroganoff sauce and sprinkle with chopped parsley before serving.

Preparation time: 10 minutes
Cooking time: 10 minutes

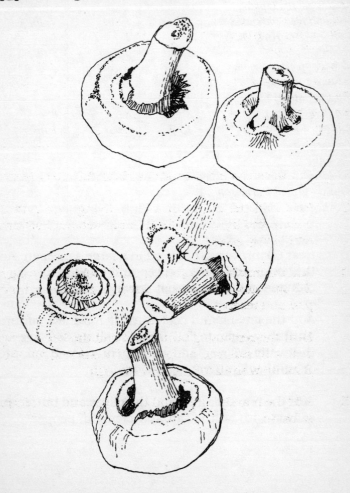

SMOKED PORK SAUSAGE AND GREENS

Ring the changes with chorizo or other spiced sausages.

Serves 4	Metric	Imperial	American
Olive oil	90 ml	6 tbsp	6 tbsp
Leeks, sliced	2	2	2
Garlic cloves, crushed	2	2	2
Spring greens (spring cabbage), shredded	350 g	12 oz	3/4 lb
Smoked pork ring, sliced	1	1	1
Water	45 ml	3 tbsp	3 tbsp
Salt and freshly ground black pepper			
Stoned (pitted) black olives, sliced	8	8	8
Butter	15 g	1/2 oz	1 tbsp
To garnish			
Cayenne			
To serve			
Freshly grated Parmesan cheese			

1. Heat 60 ml/4 tbsp of the oil in a large saucepan. Add the leeks and garlic, cover and cook gently for 5 minutes until soft but not brown.

2. Add the greens and cook stirring for a few minutes until they begin to 'fall'. Add the sliced sausage and the water. Cover and cook gently for 5 minutes or until soft, stirring occasionally.

3. Add the remaining oil and the olives and butter and season with a little salt and plenty of pepper.

Serving suggestion

Add to cooked penne, rigatoni or other macaroni, toss well and sprinkle with a little cayenne before serving with grated Parmesan cheese.

 Preparation time: 10 minutes
Cooking time: 10 minutes

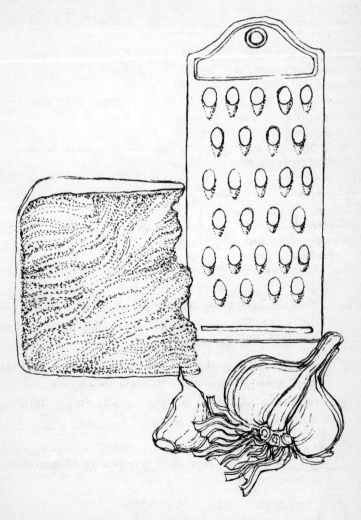

Sweet-cured Ham and Peas

This is best made with chunky bits of ham rather than thin slices. So ask at your local delicatessen counter for 'ham pieces' – the offcuts from the end of joints. They make this a very inexpensive dish indeed.

Serves 4	Metric	Imperial	American
Cooked ham pieces	225 g	8 oz	2 cups
Onion, finely chopped	2	2	2
Butter	100 g	4 oz	1/2 cup
Olive oil	15 ml	1 tbsp	1 tbsp
Frozen peas	100 g	4 oz	1 cup
Freshly grated Parmesan cheese	50 g	2 oz	1/2 cup
Salt and freshly ground black pepper			
To garnish			
A little olive oil			
To serve			
Extra freshly grated Parmesan cheese			

1. Cut the ham into very small dice, discarding any fat.

2. Fry (sauté) the onion gently in half the butter and the oil until soft but not brown.

3. Add the ham and peas, cover, reduce heat and cook gently for 5 minutes, stirring occasionally.

4. Add the remaining butter, the cheese, a very little salt and lots of pepper.

Serving suggestion
Add to cooked penne. Toss well, drizzle with a little olive oil and serve with Parmesan cheese.

 Preparation time: 5 minutes
Cooking time: 8 minutes

NEAPOLITAN BACON AND TOMATO

This is ideal for a quick supper dish. Add mushrooms if you have any in the fridge.

Serves 4	Metric	Imperial	American
Onion, chopped	1	1	1
Garlic clove, crushed	1	1	1
Olive oil	15 ml	1 tbsp	1 tbsp
Streaky bacon rashers (slices), rinded and diced	8	8	8
Can chopped tomatoes	400 g	14 oz	1 large can
Dried thyme	5 ml	1 tsp	1 tsp
Tomato purée (paste)	15 ml	1 tbsp	1 tbsp
Caster (superfine) sugar	1.5 ml	$^1/_4$ tsp	$^1/_4$ tsp
Salt and freshly ground black pepper			
To serve			
Grated Cheddar cheese			

1.   Fry (sauté) the onion and garlic in the oil until softened but not browned.

2.   Add the diced bacon and fry, stirring for 2 minutes.

3.   Add the remaining ingredients, bring to the boil, reduce heat and simmer until pulpy, about 10 minutes.

Serving suggestion

Add to any cooked pasta shapes, toss well and serve with grated Cheddar cheese.

Preparation time: 5 minutes
Cooking time: 15 minutes

SPICY MEATBALL SAUCE

For a plainer version, omit the chilli, coriander and cumin and add 5 ml/1 tsp dried oregano to the meat mixture instead.

Serves 4	Metric	Imperial	American
Minced (ground) lamb or beef	450 g	1 lb	4 cups
Onion, finely chopped	1	1	1
Garlic clove, crushed (optional)	1	1	1
Fresh breadcrumbs	50 g	2 oz	1 cup
Chilli powder	1.5 ml	$^1/_4$ tsp	$^1/_4$ tsp
Ground coriander (cilantro)	1.5 ml	$^1/_4$ tsp	$^1/_4$ tsp
Ground cumin	1.5 ml	$^1/_4$ tsp	$^1/_4$ tsp
Salt and freshly ground black pepper			
Egg (size 4) beaten	1	1	1
Oil for frying			
Jar passata (sieved tomatoes)	550 g	$1^1/_4$ lb	1 large jar
Dried oregano	5 ml	1 tsp	1 tsp
To serve			
Freshly grated Parmesan cheese			

1. Mix the meat, onion, garlic, breadcrumbs, spices and a little salt and pepper thoroughly in a bowl.

2. Add the beaten egg and mix well to bind. Shape into small balls.

3. Fry (sauté) in hot oil until golden brown, about 3 minutes. Drain on kitchen paper.

4. Pour passata into a saucepan. Add the oregano and meatballs. Simmer for 10 minutes, gently stirring occasionally.

Serving suggestion

Pile on to a plate of cooked spaghetti and top with grated Parmesan cheese.

Preparation time: 15 minutes
Cooking time: 13 minutes

PAPRIKASH SAUCE

You can use up leftover roast lamb or pork in this sauce for a Monday treat. Simply add it with the paprika and continue as below.

Serves 4	Metric	Imperial	American
Oil	15 ml	1 tbsp	1 tbsp
Onion, chopped	1	1	1
Pork or lamb fillet, finely diced	225 g	8 oz	¹/₂ lb
Paprika	15 ml	1 tbsp	1 tbsp
Can pimientos, drained and sliced	190 g	6 ³/₄ oz	1 small can
Chicken stock	150 ml	¹/₄ pt	²/₃ cup
Pinch of light brown sugar			
Salt and white pepper			
Plain (all-purpose) flour	15 ml	1 tbsp	1 tbsp
Water	15 ml	1 tbsp	1 tbsp
Soured (dairy sour) cream	150 ml	¹/₄ pt	²/₃ cup
To garnish			
Crisp fried onion rings			

1.   Heat the oil in a saucepan and fry (sauté) the onion until soft but not brown.

2.   Add the meat and cook, stirring, for 4 minutes.

3.   Add the paprika and fry for 1 minute.

4.   Add the pimientos and stock. Season with the sugar and a little salt and pepper.

5.   Bring to the boil, reduce heat, half cover and simmer gently for 15 minutes.

6. Blend the flour with the water and stir into the pan. Cook, stirring for 2 minutes. Stir in the cream and heat through. Taste and re-season if necessary.

Serving suggestion
Spoon over any cooked flat noodles and garnish with crisp fried onion rings.

Preparation time: 5 minutes
Cooking time: 25 minutes

SWEET AND SOUR CHICKEN SAUCE

Use pork instead of chicken if you prefer.

Serves 4	Metric	Imperial	American
Sunflower oil	15 ml	1 tbsp	1 tbsp
Chicken breast fillets, cut in small, thin strips	2	2	2
Carrot, cut in matchsticks	1	1	1
Small red (bell) pepper, cut in thin strips	1/2	1/2	1/2
Cucumber, diced	1/4	1/4	1/4
Can pineapple pieces	430 g	15 1/2 oz	1 large can
Tomato purée (paste)	30 ml	2 tbsp	2 tbsp
Soy sauce	45 ml	3 tbsp	3 tbsp
Ground ginger	2.5 ml	1/2 tsp	1/2 tsp
Malt vinegar	60 ml	4 tbsp	4 tbsp
Cornflour (cornstarch)	10 ml	2 tsp	2 tsp
Water	15 ml	1 tbsp	1 tbsp
To serve			
Extra soy sauce			

1. Heat the oil in a large saucepan. Fry (sauté) the chicken in the oil for 4 minutes until cooked through. Remove from the pan.

2. Add the remaining ingredients except the cornflour and water. Bring to the boil and boil for 5 minutes.

3. Blend the cornflour with the water and stir into the sauce. Cook stirring until thickened and clear. Return the chicken to the sauce and heat through.

Serving suggestion
Cook Chinese egg noodles according to the packet. Drain. Add to sweet and sour sauce, toss well and serve with extra soy sauce.

Preparation time: 15 minutes
Cooking time: 12 minutes

TURKEY VERONIQUE SAUCE

You can, of course, use chicken instead of turkey if you prefer. The only accompaniment needed is a green salad.

Serves 4	Metric	Imperial	American
Chicken stock	300 ml	1/2 pt	1 1/4 cups
Bay leaf	1	1	1
Butter	40 g	1 1/2 oz	3 tbsp
Turkey stir-fry meat	225 g	8 oz	2 cups
Plain (all-purpose) flour	25 g	1 oz	1/4 cup
Grated lemon rind	5 ml	1 tsp	1 tsp
Single (light) cream	150 ml	1/4 pt	2/3 cup
Seedless (pitless) white grapes, halved	75 g	3 oz	1/2 cup
Salt and white pepper			
To garnish			
Chopped parsley			

1.   Put the stock in a pan. Add the bay leaf. Bring to the boil and leave to infuse while preparing the rest of the sauce.

2.   Melt the butter in a separate pan. Add the turkey and cook, stirring for 4-5 minutes until cooked through.

3.   Add the flour and cook, stirring for 1 minute.

4.   Discard the bay leaf then gradually blend the stock into the turkey mixture, stirring all the time. Add the lemon rind. Bring to the boil and cook for 3 minutes, stirring.

5.   Stir in the cream, add the grapes and season to taste.

Serving suggestion
Add to any cooked pasta shapes. Toss well and sprinkle with chopped parsley before serving.

Preparation time: 5 minutes
Cooking time: 10 minutes

CHOW MEIN SAUCE

This is a basic sauce for a quick supper. Add strips of leftover chicken or pork or a handful of prawns to it for a more substantial dish.

Serves 4	Metric	Imperial	American
Sunflower oil	45 ml	3 tbsp	3 tbsp
Spring onions (scallions), trimmed and cut in 2.5 cm/1 in lengths	8	8	8
Streaky bacon rashers (slices), rinded and cut in thin strips	6	6	6
Celery sticks, cut in matchsticks	2	2	2
Button mushrooms, sliced	100 g	4 oz	2 cups
Canned bamboo shoots, cut in matchsticks	100 g	4 oz	1/4 lb
Soy sauce	45 ml	3 tbsp	3 tbsp
Chicken stock	150 ml	1/4 pt	2/3 cup
Cornflour (cornstarch)	5 ml	1 tsp	1 tsp
Dry sherry	15 ml	1 tbsp	1 tbsp
To serve			
A little butter			
Prawn crackers			

1. Heat oil in a large saucepan. Add the spring onions and bacon and fry (sauté) stirring for 2 minutes.

2. Add the celery and mushrooms and fry for a further 2 minutes, stirring.

3. Add the bamboo shoots, soy sauce and chicken stock. Bring to the boil, half cover and simmer gently for 5 minutes.

4.   Blend the cornflour with the sherry and stir into the sauce. Simmer, stirring for 1 minute.

Serving suggestion

Fry cooked chow mein noodles or spaghetti in a little butter for 2-3 minutes, stirring. Add to the sauce and simmer for 3-5 minutes before serving with prawn crackers.

 Preparation time: 15 minutes
Cooking time: 10 minutes

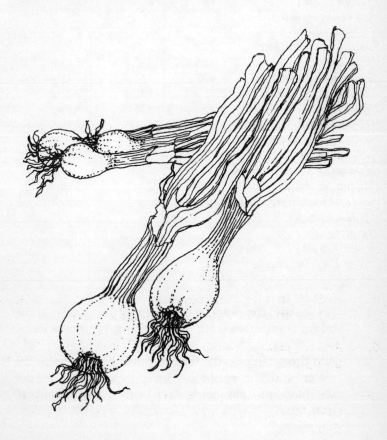

RED PEPPER, SALAMI AND MORTADELLA SAUCE

If you don't like spicy food, omit the red chilli from the recipe.

Serves 4	Metric	Imperial	American
Red onions, sliced	2	2	2
Red (bell) pepper, cut in thin strips	1	1	1
Red chilli, seeded and thinly sliced	1	1	1
Garlic clove, crushed	1	1	1
Olive oil	45 ml	3 tbsp	3 tbsp
Can chopped tomatoes	400 g	14 oz	1 large can
Tomato purée (paste)	15 ml	1 tbsp	1 tbsp
Water	45 ml	3 tbsp	3 tbsp
Dried oregano	5 ml	1 tsp	1 tsp
Stuffed green olives, sliced (optional)	8	8	8
Mortadella sausage, diced	50 g	2 oz	1/2 cup
Milano salami, diced	50 g	2 oz	1/2 cup
Salt and freshly ground black pepper			
To serve			
Freshly grated Parmesan or Pecorino cheese			

1. Fry (sauté) the onion, pepper, chilli and garlic in the oil for 3 minutes until softened but not browned.

2. Add the tomatoes, the tomato purée blended with the water and the oregano. Bring to the boil, reduce the heat and simmer gently until pulpy, about 10 minutes.

3. Add the olives, if using, and the diced sausages and cook for a further 2 minutes. Season to taste with salt, if necessary, and plenty of black pepper.

Serving suggestion
Spoon over cooked spaghetti or spaghettini and sprinkle with grated Parmesan or Pecorino cheese before serving.

 Preparation time: 10 minutes
Cooking time: 15 minutes

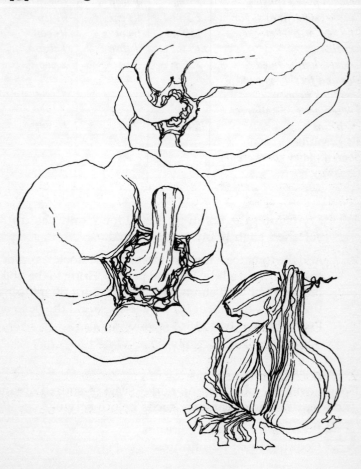

LAMB GOULASH SAUCE

Try this with leftover pork, chicken or turkey too.

Serves 4	Metric	Imperial	American
Onion, chopped	1	1	1
Oil	15 ml	1 tbsp	1 tbsp
Can chopped tomatoes	400 g	14 oz	1 large can
Tomato purée (paste)	15 ml	1 tbsp	1 tbsp
Caster (superfine) sugar	2.5 ml	¹/₂ tsp	¹/₂ tsp
Chicken or beef stock	150 ml	¹/₄ pt	²/₃ cup
Paprika	15 ml	1 tbsp	1 tbsp
Cooked lamb, diced	225 g	8 oz	2 cups
Salt and freshly ground black pepper			
Frozen peas or cut green beans	50 g	2 oz	¹/₂ cup
To garnish			
Soured (dairy sour) cream			
Caraway seeds			

1. Fry (sauté) the onion in the oil for 2 minutes until softened slightly but not browned.

2. Add the tomatoes, tomato purée, sugar, stock, paprika, the lamb, and a little salt and pepper. Bring to the boil, reduce heat, and simmer gently for about 30 minutes until pulpy and meat is really tender. Add the peas or beans for last 5 minutes cooking time.

3. Taste and re-season if necessary.

Serving suggestion
Spoon over flat noodles and add a swirl of soured cream and a sprinkling of caraway seeds before serving.

Preparation time: 5 minutes
Cooking time: 32 minutes

CHICKEN WITH LEEKS AND WALNUTS

An interesting combination of textures and flavours.

Serves 4	Metric	Imperial	American
Small leeks, thinly sliced	2	2	2
Walnut oil	15 ml	1 tbsp	1 tbsp
Olive oil	15 ml	1 tbsp	1 tbsp
Walnuts, roughly chopped	50 g	2 oz	1/2 cup
Chicken breast fillets, finely diced	2	2	2
Medium dry white wine	150 ml	1/4 pt	2/3 cup
Crème fraîche	150 ml	1/4 pt	2/3 cup
Salt and freshly ground black pepper			
To garnish			
Chopped parsley			

1   Fry (sauté) the leeks in the two types of oil for 2 minutes until slightly softened. Add the walnuts, cover with a lid, reduce heat and cook gently for 5 minutes until soft.

2.   Add the chicken and wine, re-cover and simmer gently for 10 minutes until chicken is tender.

3.   Stir in the crème fraîche and season to taste.

Serving suggestion
Spoon over cooked vermicelli and sprinkle with chopped parsley before serving.

Preparation time: 8 minutes
Cooking time: 18 minutes

TANGY HAM, RAISIN AND PINE NUT SAUCE

The salty flavour of the Feta cheese offsets the richness of the sauce in this unusual dish.

Serves 4	Metric	Imperial	American
Butter	25 g	1 oz	2 tbsp
Onion, chopped	1	1	1
Small green (bell) pepper, diced	1	1	1
Celery sticks, diced	2	2	2
Carrot, diced	1	1	1
Raisins	40 g	1¹/₂ oz	¹/₄ cup
Tomato purée (paste)	30 ml	2 tbsp	2 tbsp
Ham or chicken stock	300 ml	¹/₂ pt	1¹/₄ cups
Cooked ham, diced	175 g	6 oz	1¹/₂ cups
Pine nuts	25 g	1 oz	¹/₄ cup
Cornflour (cornstarch)	10 ml	2 tsp	2 tsp
White wine vinegar	15 ml	1 tbsp	1 tbsp
To serve			
Crumbled Feta cheese			

1. Melt the butter in a large saucepan. Add the onion, pepper and celery and cook gently, stirring for 5 minutes until softened but not browned.

2. Add the remaining ingredients except the cornflour and vinegar. Bring to the boil, reduce heat and simmer gently for 20 minutes.

3. Blend the cornflour with the vinegar. Stir into the sauce and cook until thickened and clear.

Serving suggestion

Spoon over cooked bucatini or other long macaroni or spaghetti and top with the crumbled Feta cheese.

 Preparation time: 10 minutes
Cooking time: 26 minutes

Simple Supper Sauce

Ring the changes with different hard cheeses.

Serves 4	Metric	Imperial	American
Streaky bacon rashers (slices), diced	*4*	*4*	*4*
Red Leicester cheese, grated	*100 g*	*4 oz*	*1 cup*
Worcestershire sauce	*5 ml*	*1 tsp*	*1 tsp*
Salt and freshly ground black pepper			
Butter	*25 g*	*1 oz*	*2 tbsp*
Snipped chives	*15 ml*	*1 tbsp*	*1 tbsp*

1.   Dry-fry (sauté) the bacon until crisp. Drain on kitchen paper and leave to garnish dish before serving

2.   Mix in the cheese, Worcestershire sauce, a little salt and pepper and the butter cut in small flakes.

Serving suggestion
Add the cheese mixture to cooked macaroni. Toss over a gentle heat until melted then spoon into warm bowls and garnish with the bacon and chives.

 Preparation time: 3 minutes
Cooking time: 5 minutes

SEAFOOD SAUCES

Pasta goes well with just about every kind of fish and shellfish from good old canned tuna to more exotic smoked salmon.

Seafood Cocktail and Fennel Sauce

A wonderful starter for 8 people or an excellent main course for a supper party.

Serves 4	Metric	Imperial	American
Fennel bulb	1	1	1
Olive oil	45 ml	3 tbsp	3 tbsp
Spring onions (scallions), chopped	8	8	8
White wine	30 ml	2 tbsp	2 tbsp
Frozen seafood cocktail, thawed	225 g	8 oz	1/2 lb
Salt and freshly ground black pepper			
To garnish			
Lemon twists			

1. Finely chop the fennel, reserving the green fronds for garnish.

2. Heat the oil in a saucepan. Add the chopped fennel and spring onions and cook, stirring for 3 minutes. Cover with a lid and cook gently for 5 minutes until softened.

3. Add the wine and the seafood. Bring to the boil, reduce heat and cook gently, stirring until hot through, about 3 minutes. Season to taste with salt and pepper.

Serving suggestion
Toss with multi-coloured cooked tagliatelle and garnish with twists of lemon and the reserved fennel fronds before serving.

Preparation time: 5 minutes
Cooking time: 11 minutes

TUSCAN TUNA AND BEAN SAUCE

This is a great way of making a little tuna go a long way. It is also very good served cold, spiked with a dash of wine vinegar.

Serves 6	Metric	Imperial	American
Olive oil	250 ml	8 fl oz	1 cup
Lemon juice	100 ml	3¹/₂ fl oz	6¹/₂ tbsp
Garlic cloves, crushed	2	2	2
Can cannellini beans, drained	2 × 425 g	2 × 15 oz	2 large cans
Chopped parsley	30 ml	2 tbsp	2 tbsp
Can tuna, drained	185 g	6¹/₂ oz	1 small can
Salt and freshly ground black pepper			
To garnish			
A few black olives, stoned (pitted)			
Snipped chives			

1. Mix the oil, lemon juice, garlic, cannellini beans and parsley together in a saucepan. Cook for 5 minutes, stirring occasionally until hot through.

2. Gently fold in the tuna and a little salt and pepper and heat through, taking care to break up the tuna chunks.

Serving suggestion
Add to any short cut macaroni, toss gently and serve garnished with a few black olives and some snipped chives.

 Preparation time: 3 minutes
Cooking time: 8 minutes

CHEESY TUNA AND SWEETCORN

A store-cupboard favourite with all the family.

Serves 4	Metric	Imperial	American
Plain (all-purpose) flour	20 g	$3/4$ oz	3 tbsp
Butter	20 g	$3/4$ oz	$1^1/2$ tbsp
Milk	300 ml	$1/2$ pt	$1^1/4$ cups
Strong Cheddar cheese, grated	50 g	2 oz	$1/2$ cup
Salt and freshly ground black pepper			
Can tuna, drained	185 g	$6^1/2$ oz	1 small can
Can sweetcorn (corn), drained	200 g	7 oz	1 small can
Chopped parsley	15 ml	1 tbsp	1 tbsp
To garnish			
Garlic croûtons			

1. Whisk the flour, butter and milk together in a saucepan until the flour is well blended in.

2. Bring to the boil, stirring all the time, until thickened and smooth. Simmer for 2 minutes.

3. Add the remaining ingredients and heat through, stirring until piping hot.

Serving suggestion

Toss with cooked conchiglie or other pasta shapes and sprinkle with garlic croûtons before serving.

Preparation time: 5 minutes
Cooking time: 5 minutes

OLYMPIAN TUNA AND TOMATO

A simple full-flavoured sauce with a little twist in the serving.

Serves 4	Metric	Imperial	American
Garlic clove, crushed	1	1	1
Chicken stock	150 ml	1/4 pt	2/3 cup
Can chopped tomatoes	200 g	7 oz	1 small can
Tomato purée (paste)	15 ml	1 tbsp	1 tbsp
Snipped chives	30 ml	2 tbsp	2 tbsp
Dry vermouth	45 ml	3 tbsp	3 tbsp
Cornflour (cornstarch)	10 ml	2 tsp	2 tsp
Water	15 ml	1 tbsp	1 tbsp
Can tuna, drained	185 g	6 1/2 oz	1 small can
Salt and freshly ground black pepper			
Olive oil	15 ml	1 tbsp	1 tbsp
To garnish			
Single (light) cream	30 ml	2 tbsp	2 tbsp

1. Place the garlic, stock, tomatoes, tomato purée, chives and vermouth in a saucepan. Bring to the boil, reduce heat and simmer for 5 minutes or until reduced by half.

2. Add the tuna and heat through, stirring.

3. Blend the cornflour with the water. Add to the sauce, bring to the boil and simmer for 1 minute, stirring.

4. Season to taste and stir in the olive oil.

Serving suggestion

Toss any cooked ribbon pasta in the single cream and heat through gently. Sprinkle well with black pepper. Pile on to plates and spoon the sauce on top.

 Preparation time: 3 minutes
Cooking time: 8 minutes

SALSA DI VONGOLE

Baby clams are readily available in cans. Cockles can be used instead, but take care they have not been pickled in vinegar. This version is a 'white' sauce but you can also add clams to a garlic-flavoured tomato sauce (see page 100) for an equally authentic 'Salsa di Vongole'.

Serves 4-6	Metric	Imperial	American
Butter	40 g	1¹/₂ oz	3 tbsp
Olive oil	15 ml	1 tbsp	1 tbsp
Garlic cloves, crushed	3	3	3
Dry white wine	100 ml	3¹/₂ fl oz	6¹/₂ tbsp
Can baby clams	2 × 295 g	2 × 10³/₄ oz	2 small cans
Freshly ground black pepper			
To garnish			
Chopped parsley			

1. Melt the butter with the oil in a saucepan. Add the garlic and cook gently for 2 minutes until lightly golden but not too brown.

2. Add the wine, bring to the boil and simmer for 2 minutes until slightly reduced.

3. Drain the clams, reserving the juice. Add the clams and 45 ml/3 tbsp of their juice to the saucepan. Heat through gently until piping hot.

Serving suggestion
Spoon over spaghettini and sprinkle with chopped parsley. Cheese is not served with this dish.

Preparation time: 3 minutes
Cooking time: 6 minutes

SARDINIAN CLAMS WITH BACON

To give the dish a more authentic taste, use Pancetta (Italian pink and white fat bacon) instead of good old English rashers. You probably won't need any salt, but taste just before serving and add a little if necessary.

Serves 4	Metric	Imperial	American
Bunch of spring onions (scallions), chopped	1	1	1
Carrot, finely diced	1	1	1
Olive oil	150 ml	1/4 pt	2/3 cup
Garlic cloves, crushed	2	2	2
Streaky bacon rashers (slices), diced	4	4	4
Can baby clams, drained	2 x 295 g	2 x 10³/4 oz	2 small cans
Pinch of cayenne			
Chopped thyme	10 ml	2 tsp	2 tsp
Freshly ground black pepper			
To garnish			
Chopped parsley			

1. Fry (sauté) the onions and carrot in 60 ml/4 tbsp of the oil for 3 minutes until softened but not browned.

2. Add the garlic and bacon and continue cooking for a further 3 minutes, stirring.

3. Add the remaining oil with the clams, cayenne, thyme and a good grinding of pepper. Heat through gently, stirring, until piping hot.

Serving suggestion

Add to cooked fusilli. Toss well over a gentle heat. Garnish with chopped parsley before serving.

Preparation time: 15 minutes
Cooking time: 10 minutes

FIERY MUSSEL SAUCE

This recipe has its roots firmly in Northern Spain where mussels bathed in a hot tomato sauce are a favourite tapas.

Serves 4	Metric	Imperial	American
Olive oil	30 ml	2 tbsp	2 tbsp
Onion, finely chopped	1	1	1
Garlic clove, crushed	1	1	1
Fresh red chilli, seeded and chopped	1	1	1
Canned pimiento caps, roughly chopped	2	2	2
Can chopped tomatoes	400 g	14 oz	1 large can
Tomato purée (paste)	15 ml	1 tbsp	1 tbsp
Can mussels, drained	250 g	9 oz	1 small can
Salt and freshly ground black pepper			

1. Heat the oil in a saucepan. Add the onion and garlic and cook gently for 2 minutes until softened but not browned.

2. Add the chilli, pimientos, tomatoes and tomato purée. Bring to the boil, reduce heat and simmer gently for 10 minutes until pulpy.

3. Stir in the mussels. Season to taste and heat through gently until piping hot.

Serving suggestion
Spoon over cooked vermicelli and toss well before serving.

Preparation time: 10 minutes
Cooking time: 14 minutes

MUSSEL PERFECTION

If you are not keen on garlic, use a finely chopped onion instead.

Serves 4–6	Metric	Imperial	American
Mussels in their shells	2 kg	4¹/₂ lb	4¹/₂ lb
Olive oil	120 ml	4 fl oz	¹/₂ cup
Garlic cloves, crushed	3	3	3
Chicken stock	150 ml	¹/₄ pt	²/₃ cup
Brandy	15 ml	1 tbsp	1 tbsp
Chopped parsley	30 ml	2 tbsp	2 tbsp
Salt and freshly ground black pepper			

1. Scrub the mussels, discard the beards and any shells that are damaged, open or won't close when sharply tapped.

2. Heat 45 ml/3 tbsp of oil in a large pan. Add the garlic and fry (sauté) gently until golden.

3. Add the mussels and the stock. Cover and cook gently for 3–4 minutes, shaking the pan occasionally until the mussels have opened.

4. Strain the liquid into a clean pan. Carefully remove mussels from their shells and add to the liquid.

5. Stir in the brandy and parsley and season to taste. Reheat gently.

Serving suggestion
Add cooked vermicelli to the sauce. Heat through tossing gently.

Preparation time: 20 minutes
Cooking time: 8 minutes

CAVIAR-TOPPED PRAWN WITH ARTICHOKE SAUCE

Don't add salt to this sauce. The olives and lumpfish roe season it perfectly.

Serves 4	Metric	Imperial	American
Olive oil	45 ml	3 tbsp	3 tbsp
Onion, finely chopped	1	1	1
Dry white vermouth	45 ml	3 tbsp	3 tbsp
Can artichoke hearts, drained and chopped	425 g	15 oz	1 large can
Peeled prawns (shrimp)	100 g	4 oz	1 cup
Green olives, stoned (pitted) and halved	6	6	6
Freshly ground black pepper			
Snipped chives	15 ml	1 tbsp	1 tbsp
To garnish			
Danish lumpfish roe	50 g	2 oz	$^1/_4$ cup

1. Heat the oil in a saucepan. Add the onion and fry (sauté) gently for 3 minutes until softened but not browned.

2. Add the vermouth, bring to the boil and simmer for 1 minute.

3. Add the artichokes, prawns, olives and a good grinding of pepper. Heat through, stirring gently until piping hot. Add the chives.

Serving suggestion
Spoon over farfalle, toss well and serve each portion with a spoonful of lumpfish roe on top.

Preparation time: 10 minutes
Cooking time: 7 minutes

CIDERED PRAWNS WITH COURGETTES

This recipe is also good with diced crabsticks instead of the prawns.

Serves 4-6	Metric	Imperial	American
Butter	50 g	2 oz	¼ cup
Bunch of spring onions (scallions), chopped	1	1	1
Courgettes (zucchini), sliced	2	2	2
Fish stock	450 ml	¾ pt	2 cups
Dry cider	150 ml	¼ pt	⅔ cup
Cornflour (cornstarch)	30 ml	2 tbsp	2 tbsp
Peeled prawns (shrimp)	175 g	6 oz	1½ cups
Chopped parsley	15 ml	1 tbsp	1 tbsp
Salt and white pepper			
Single (light) cream	150 ml	¼ pt	⅔ cup

1. Melt the butter in a saucepan. Add the spring onions and courgettes and fry (sauté) gently for 2 minutes. Cover and cook for 5 minutes until softened but not browned, stirring occasionally.

2. Add the stock and bring to the boil. Simmer for 2 minutes.

3. Blend the cider with the cornflour and stir into the mixture. Bring to the boil and simmer for 1 minute, stirring all the time.

4. Stir in the prawns, parsley, a little salt and pepper and the cream. Heat through gently, until piping hot.

Serving suggestion
Spoon over cooked lumachi and serve.

 Preparation time: 10 minutes
Cooking time: 11 minutes

CHINESE-STYLE PRAWNS WITH CUCUMBER SAUCE

To make the dish serve 6 people, add 100 g/4 oz/1 cup bean sprouts with the cucumber then continue as in the recipe.

Serves 4	Metric	Imperial	American
Cucumber, diced	1	1	1
Butter	50 g	2 oz	1/4 cup
Button mushrooms, sliced	175 g	6 oz	3 cups
Plain (all-purpose) flour	15 ml	1 tbsp	1 tbsp
Chicken stock	150 ml	1/4 pt	2/3 cup
Medium-dry sherry	15 ml	1 tbsp	1 tbsp
Grated fresh root ginger (ginger root)	5 ml	1 tsp	1 tsp
Single (light) cream	90 ml	6 tbsp	6 tbsp
Peeled prawns (shrimp)	175 g	6 oz	1 1/2 cups
Salt and white pepper			

1. Boil the cucumber in lightly salted water for 3 minutes. Drain, rinse with cold water and drain again.

2. Melt the butter in the same saucepan. Add the mushrooms and cook for 2 minutes, stirring.

3. Add the cucumber, cover and cook for a further 3 minutes.

4. Stir in the flour then the stock, sherry, ginger and cream. Bring to the boil and cook for 2 minutes, stirring.

5. Add the prawns, heat through until piping hot and season to taste.

Serving suggestion

Spoon over cooked Chinese egg or wheat noodles, toss and serve. Alternatively, omit the flour, add soaked cellophane noodles with the stock, sherry and ginger. Do not add the cream at this stage. Simmer the noodles until cooked, adding a little more stock if necessary. Then add the cream and prawns, heat through and season to taste.

 Preparation time: 10 minutes
Cooking time: 12 minutes

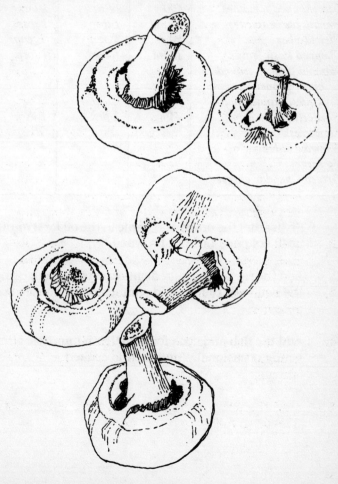

COD RAGU

Use any white fish fillet for this easy-to-make sauce.

Serves 4-6	Metric	Imperial	American
Onion, chopped	1	1	1
Garlic clove, crushed	1	1	1
Olive oil	15 ml	1 tbsp	1 tbsp
Button mushrooms, sliced	100 g	4 oz	2 cups
Can chopped tomatoes	400 g	14 oz	1 large can
Tomato purée (paste)	15 ml	1 tbsp	1 tbsp
Shelled peas	50 g	2 oz	1/2 cup
Chopped basil leaves	15 ml	1 tbsp	1 tbsp
Salt and freshly ground black pepper			
Cod fillet, skinned and diced	450 g	1 lb	1 lb
To garnish			
A few basil leaves			
To serve			
Grated Cheddar cheese			

1. Fry (sauté) the onion and garlic in the oil for 2 minutes until softened but not browned.

2. Add the remaining ingredients except the cod. Bring to the boil, reduce heat and simmer for 10 minutes until pulpy.

3. Add the fish and cook for a further 5 minutes, stirring gently occasionally until fish is cooked.

Serving suggestion

Spoon over cooked pappardelle, garnish with a few basil leaves and serve with grated Cheddar cheese.

This sauce also makes a good base for a lasagne (see page 17).

 Preparation time: 10 minutes
Cooking time: 17 minutes

SALT COD WITH CAPERS, GHERKINS AND OLIVES

Remember to soak the cod for 24 hours before use.

Serves 4	Metric	Imperial	American
Salt cod, soaked in cold water overnight	450 g	1 lb	1 lb
Lemon juice	15 ml	1 tbsp	1 tbsp
Plain (all-purpose) flour	50 g	2 oz	½ cup
Oil for shallow frying			
Olive oil	15 ml	1 tbsp	1 tbsp
Garlic clove, crushed	1	1	1
Onion, chopped	1	1	1
Can chopped tomatoes	400 g	14 oz	1 large can
Tomato purée (paste)	15 g	1 tbsp	1 tbsp
Caster (superfine) sugar	5 ml	1 tsp	1 tsp
Green stuffed olives	12	12	12
Cocktail gherkins (cornichons), halved lengthways	6	6	6
Capers	10 ml	2 tsp	2 tsp
Chopped parsley	15 ml	1 tbsp	1 tbsp

1. Drain soaked cod. Place in a saucepan and cover with cold water and lemon juice. Bring to the boil, part-cover and boil for 5 minutes. Drain and repeat until fish is tender.

2. Remove skin and any bones and break fish into bite-sized pieces. Dust with flour. Shallow fry until golden brown. Drain on kitchen paper.

3. Meanwhile heat the olive oil in a saucepan. Fry (sauté) the garlic and onion for 3 minutes until soft but not brown. Add the tomatoes, tomato purée and sugar. Bring to the boil, reduce heat and simmer for 10 minutes until pulpy.

4. Stir in the cod, olives, gherkins and capers. Simmer gently for 3 minutes. Stir in the parsley.

Serving suggestion
Spoon over cooked zite or other large pasta tubes and serve very hot.

 Preparation time: 8 minutes, plus soaking time
Cooking time: 30 minutes

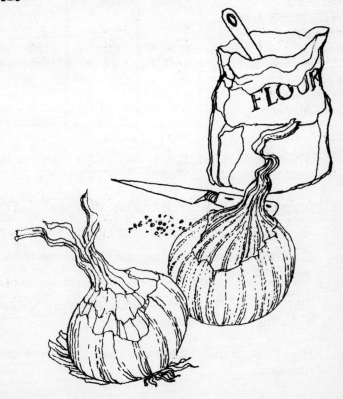

BRANDIED CRAB SAUCE

Crab Thermidor is a very rich dish. Serving the mixture as a sauce with pasta offsets this and makes it a perfect party dish.

Serves 4-6	Metric	Imperial	American
Plain (all-purpose) flour	25 g	1 oz	¼ cup
Butter	25 g	1 oz	2 tbsp
Milk	300 ml	½ pt	1¼ cups
Single (light) cream	30 ml	2 tbsp	2 tbsp
Cheddar cheese, grated	50 g	2 oz	½ cup
Dijon mustard	5 ml	1 tsp	1 tsp
Dried thyme	2.5 ml	½ tsp	½ tsp
Salt and freshly ground black pepper			
Brandy	15 ml	1 tbsp	1 tbsp
Can white crabmeat	2 × 170 g	2 × 6 oz	2 small cans
To garnish			
Toasted, buttered breadcrumbs			

1. Whisk the flour, butter, and milk together in a saucepan until the flour is blended in.

2. Bring to the boil and cook for 2 minutes, stirring all the time.

3. Stir in the cream, cheese, mustard and thyme. Season with a little salt and pepper.

4. Add the brandy and contents of both cans of crabmeat, including the juice. Stir in gently.

5. Heat through until piping hot. Taste and re-season if necessary.

Serving suggestion

Spoon over any cooked pasta shapes. Sprinkle with toasted, buttered breadcrumbs before serving.

 Preparation time: 5 minutes
Cooking time: 8 minutes

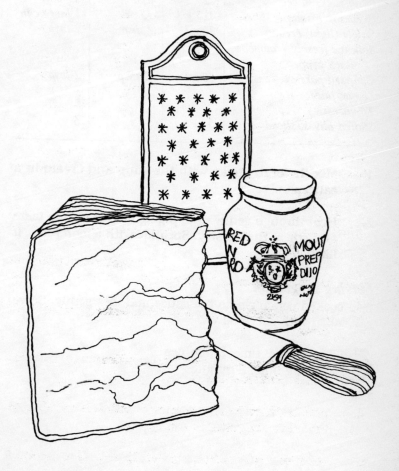

QUICK CRAB CREATION

This dish tastes equally delicious with prawns (shrimp) instead of crab sticks.

Serves 4	Metric	Imperial	American
Crab sticks, diced	225 g	8 oz	1/2 lb
Can crab bisque	425 g	15 oz	1 large can
Single (light) cream	30 ml	2 tbsp	2 tbsp
Salt and freshly ground black pepper			
Chopped parsley	30 ml	2 tbsp	2 tbsp
Lemon juice			
To garnish			
Stuffed olives, sliced	6	6	6

1. Mix the crab sticks with the soup and cream in a saucepan.

2. Heat through gently until piping hot. Season to taste and stir in the parsley. Sprinkle with lemon juice, if liked.

Serving suggestion
Add cooked conchiglie to the sauce and toss gently. Serve garnished with sliced olives.

 Preparation time: 3 minutes
Cooking time: 3 minutes

WELSH SCALLOP AND BACON SAUCE

Baby scallops are ideal for this dish, and are available from wet fish counters in most supermarkets. If unavailable, use 8 large scallops, cut into quarters.

Serves 4-6	Metric	Imperial	American
Small leeks, sliced	*2*	*2*	*2*
Butter	*25 g*	*1 oz*	*2 tbsp*
Fish stock	*90 ml*	*6 tbsp*	*6 tbsp*
Streaky bacon rashers (slices)	*3*	*3*	*3*
Baby scallops	*175 g*	*6 oz*	*1 cup*
Fromage frais	*50 g*	*2 oz*	*1/4 cup*
Salt and freshly ground black pepper			
To garnish			
Chopped parsley			

1. Fry (sauté) the leeks in half the butter for 2 minutes until softened but not browned.

2. Add the stock, cover and simmer gently for 5 minutes until tender. Purée in a blender or food processor then return to the saucepan.

3. Meanwhile dry-fry the bacon until the fat runs. Add the scallops and cook quickly tossing for 2 minutes until cooked through.

4. Stir the fromage frais into the leek purée. Add the bacon and scallops and stir in gently. Season to taste and heat through until piping hot.

Serving suggestion

Spoon over green tagliatelle and sprinkle with chopped parsley before serving.

Preparation time: 10 minutes
Cooking time: 12 minutes

COUNTRY COD AND VEGETABLES

Try using different mixtures of frozen vegetables in this useful store-cupboard standby.

Serves 6	Metric	Imperial	American
Fish or vegetable stock	300 ml	1/2 pt	1 1/4 cups
Tomato ketchup (catsup)	60 ml	4 tbsp	4 tbsp
Mayonnaise (not salad cream)	30 ml	2 tbsp	2 tbsp
Frozen mixed country vegetables	350 g	12 oz	3 cups
Salt and pepper			
Frozen cod fillet, thawed, skinned and cubed	450 g	1 lb	1 lb
Dried mixed herbs	2.5 ml	1/2 tsp	1/2 tsp
To serve			
Grated Cheddar cheese			

1. Mix the stock, ketchup and mayonnaise together in a saucepan. Add the vegetables and a little seasoning, cover and simmer for 10 minutes or until tender.

2. Add the fish and herbs and simmer for 5 minutes.

Serving suggestion
Spoon over cooked fettuccine and serve with grated Cheddar cheese, if liked.

 Preparation time: 3 minutes
Cooking time: 15 minutes

SALSA ALLA RUSTICA

This is one of the best sauces to complement home-made tagliatelle.

Serves 4	Metric	Imperial	American
Garlic cloves, crushed	2	2	2
Olive oil	90 ml	6 tbsp	6 tbsp
Can anchovy fillets, chopped, reserving oil	50 g	2 oz	1 small can
Dried oregano	5 ml	1 tsp	1 tsp
Salt and freshly ground black pepper			
To garnish			
Roughly chopped parsley	45 ml	3 tbsp	3 tbsp
Thinly shaved fresh Parmesan cheese (pared from a block with a potato peeler)			

1. Fry (sauté) the garlic in the oil until golden brown.

2. Remove from the heat and add the anchovies and their oil. Return to the heat and cook gently, stirring, until the anchovies form a paste.

3. Stir in the oregano, a very little salt and lots of black pepper.

Serving suggestion
Add to freshly cooked tagliatelle, toss well. Sprinkle with the parsley and the shavings of Parmesan.

Preparation time: 5 minutes
Cooking time: 6-8 minutes

Roman-style Squid and Radicchio Sauce

Serve lots of crusty bread with this dish to mop up every last drop of the colourful sauce.

Serves 4	Metric	Imperial	American
Olive oil	60 ml	4 tbsp	4 tbsp
Garlic cloves, crushed	2	2	2
Red onion, chopped	1	1	1
Green (bell) pepper, finely chopped	1/2	1/2	1/2
Baby squid, cleaned and sliced into rings	450 g	1 lb	1 lb
Salt and freshly ground black pepper			
Lemon juice	30 ml	2 tbsp	2 tbsp
Small head radicchio, torn into bite-sized pieces	1	1	1
Chopped parsley	15 ml	1 tbsp	1 tbsp

1. Heat the oil in a large frying pan (skillet) and fry (sauté) the garlic, onion and pepper for 3 minutes, stirring until softened but not browned.

2. Add the squid, season well with salt and pepper and add the lemon juice. Stir-fry for 1 minute then cover and cook gently for 5 minutes.

3. Add the radicchio and cook stirring for 2 minutes until slightly wilted. Sprinkle with chopped parsley and heat through for a further minute.

Serving suggestion

Spoon over any cooked ribbon noodles and serve very hot.

 Preparation time: 15 minutes
Cooking time: 11 minutes

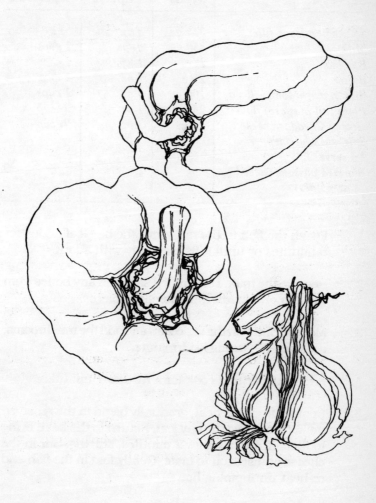

SCOTTISH SMOKED HADDOCK

You can, of course, use any smoked fish for this recipe. It is also good with plain white fish too.

Serves 4	Metric	Imperial	American
Smoked haddock fillet	225 g	8 oz	1/2 lb
Milk	450 ml	3/4 pt	2 cups
Bay leaf	1	1	1
Butter	25 g	1 oz	2 tbsp
Button mushrooms, sliced	100 g	4 oz	2 cups
Plain (all-purpose) flour	25 g	1 oz	1/4 cup
Grated Cheddar cheese	75 g	3 oz	3/4 cup
Salt and white pepper			
To serve			
Warmed passata (sieved tomatoes)			

1. Poach the fish in the milk with the bay leaf added for 5 minutes or until it flakes easily with a fork.

2. Reserve the milk. Discard the skin and any bones from the fish and break into bite-sized pieces.

3. Melt the butter in the saucepan and add the mushrooms, cook gently, stirring for 1 minute.

4. Add the flour and cook for a further 1 minute.

5. Remove from the heat, gradually blend in the reserved milk, discarding the bay leaf. Return to the heat, bring to the boil and cook for 2 minutes, stirring. Stir in the cheese and season to taste. Gently fold in the fish and re-heat until piping hot.

Serving suggestion

Spoon over cooked elbow macaroni and toss well. If liked, sprinkle with a little more grated cheese and flash under a hot grill (broiler) to brown top. Serve with warmed passata (sieved tomatoes) handed separately.

Preparation time: 5 minutes
Cooking time: 11 minutes

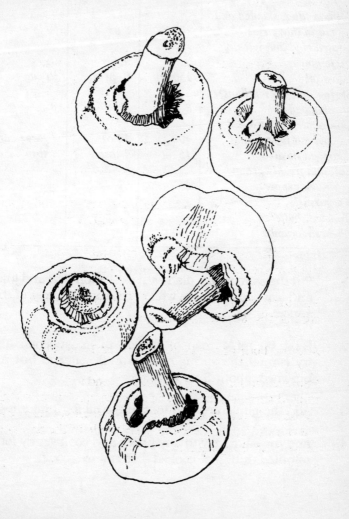

SALMON WITH PIMIENTOS AND BASIL

For a quick supper dish, use a can of salmon instead of the fillet. Take care not to break the fish up too much when you remove the skin and bones.

Serves 4	Metric	Imperial	American
Salmon fillet, skinned and cut in thin strips	225 g	8 oz	1/2 lb
Grated rind and juice of lemon	1/2	1/2	1/2
Olive oil	150 ml	1/4 pt	2/3 cup
Spring onions (scallions), chopped	8	8	8
Can pimientos, drained and cut in strips	400 g	14 oz	1 large can
Chopped basil	15 ml	1 tbsp	1 tbsp
Salt and freshly ground black pepper			
To garnish			
Toasted, buttered breadcrumbs			

1. Put the salmon in a dish with the lemon rind and juice and leave to marinate while preparing the rest of the sauce.

2. Heat 60 ml/4 tbsp of the oil in a saucepan and fry (sauté) the spring onions until softened but not browned, about 3 minutes.

3. Add the pimientos and toss in the oil for 2 minutes.

4. Add the salmon with any juices and cook gently for 2 minutes until just cooked – do not overcook.

5. Add the basil and remaining oil and season well with salt and pepper. Heat through until piping hot.

Serving suggestion
Add immediately to cooked wholewheat ruote and toss well. Serve very hot, sprinkled with the toasted breadcrumbs.

 Preparation time: 15 minutes
Cooking time: 8 minutes

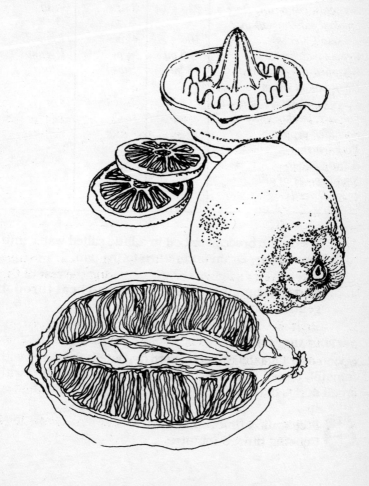

SMOKED SALMON, EGG AND BROCCOLI SAUCE

Look for smoked salmon pieces which are much cheaper than slices.

Serves 6	Metric	Imperial	American
Broccoli, cut in tiny florets	225 g	8 oz	1/2 lb
Smoked salmon, cut in small pieces	100 g	4 oz	1 cup
Crème fraîche	300 ml	1/2 pt	1 1/4 cups
Chopped dill (dillweed)	15 ml	1 tbsp	1 tbsp
Hard-boiled (hard-cooked) eggs, roughly chopped	2	2	2
Salt and freshly ground black pepper			
To garnish			
A little butter			
Small sprigs of dill (dillweed)			

1. Steam the broccoli or boil in a little salted water until just tender. Drain and return to the pan.

2. Add the remaining ingredients and heat through gently, stirring lightly until piping hot.

Serving suggestion

Spoon over tagliatelle al pomodoro (tagliatelle flavoured with tomato), tossed in a little butter, and serve garnished with small sprigs of dill.

Preparation time: 8 minutes
Cooking time: 8 minutes

VEGETABLE SAUCES

The glorious colours and flavours of vegetable sauces with pasta make them ideal as main meals in their own right, or they can be served as a starter or an accompaniment to fish or meat (when they'll serve more people). The combinations are endless and the results always rewarding.

CHILLI BEAN BONANZA

This mixture makes an excellent lasagne filling too.

Serves 4–6	Metric	Imperial	American
Onion, chopped	1	1	1
Garlic clove, crushed	1	1	1
Mushrooms, sliced	100 g	4 oz	2 cups
Small red (bell) pepper, chopped	1	1	1
Olive oil	30 ml	2 tbsp	2 tbsp
Can chopped tomatoes	400 g	14 oz	1 large can
Red chilli, seeded and chopped	1	1	1
Ground cumin	5 ml	1 tsp	1 tsp
Dried oregano	5 ml	1 tsp	1 tsp
Salt and freshly ground black pepper			
Can red kidney beans, drained	2×425 g	2×15 oz	2 large cans
To serve			
Grated Cheddar cheese			

1. Fry (sauté) the onion, garlic, mushrooms and pepper in the oil for 2 minutes, stirring.

2. Add the tomatoes, chilli, cumin, oregano and a little salt and pepper. Bring to the boil, reduce heat and simmer for 10 minutes.

3. Stir in the beans and simmer for a further 5 minutes.

Serving suggestion
Spoon over spaghetti and serve with grated Cheddar cheese.

Preparation time: 10 minutes
Cooking time: 17 minutes

PIQUANT RED LENTIL AND TOMATO SAUCE

This makes a cheap and nutritious supper dish.

Serves 4	Metric	Imperial	American
Red lentils	225 g	8 oz	1$^{1}/_{3}$ cups
Can chopped tomatoes	400 g	14 oz	1 large can
Can pimientos, drained and chopped	200 g	7 oz	1 small can
Dried mixed herbs	5 ml	1 tsp	1 tsp
Tomato purée (paste)	15 ml	1 tbsp	1 tbsp
Caster (superfine) sugar	5 ml	1 tsp	1 tsp
Tabasco sauce			
Salt and freshly ground black pepper			
Chopped parsley	15 ml	1 tbsp	1 tbsp
To garnish			
Olive oil			
Freshly grated Parmesan cheese			

1. Boil the lentils in salted water for 10 minutes, drain and return to the saucepan.

2. Add the tomatoes, pimientos, herbs, tomato purée, sugar and a good sprinkling of Tabasco. Bring to the boil and simmer for 10 minutes until pulpy.

3. Season to taste and stir in the parsley.

Serving suggestion
Toss cooked multi-coloured pasta shapes in a little olive oil. Add the sauce, toss again and serve with plenty of grated Parmesan sprinkled over.

Preparation time: 3 minutes
Cooking time: 20 minutes

RUSSIAN-STYLE LENTIL SAUCE

This unusual, colourful dish makes a hearty winter meal.
Use a food processor to do the grating for you if you have one.

Serves 4-6	Metric	Imperial	American
Onion, grated	1	1	1
Small swede (rutabaga), grated	1	1	1
Butter	50 g	2 oz	1/4 cup
Large cooked beetroot (red beet)	2	2	2
Red lentils	100 g	4 oz	2/3 cup
Vegetable stock	750 ml	1 1/4 pts	3 cups
Red wine vinegar	15 ml	1 tbsp	1 tbsp
Dried tarragon	2.5 ml	1/2 tsp	1/2 tsp
Salt and freshly ground black pepper			
To garnish			
Soured (dairy sour) cream			
Cayenne			
To serve			
Grated mature Cheddar cheese			

1. Fry (sauté) the onion and swede in the butter for 2 minutes, stirring.

2. Add the remaining ingredients, seasoning well with salt and pepper.

3. Bring to the boil, reduce heat and simmer gently for 30 minutes until vegetables are cooked through.

Serving suggestion

Add to any cooked wholewheat pasta shapes. Heat through for 5 minutes, stirring, so pasta absorbs any excess juices. Pile onto serving plates, top with a spoonful of soured (dairy sour) cream and a sprinkling of cayenne. Serve with grated cheese.

 Preparation time: 5-10 minutes
Cooking time: 32 minutes

Chick Pea Goulash Sauce

Ring the changes by adding diced green (bell) pepper, green beans or a diced courgette (zucchini) instead of peas.

Serves 4	Metric	Imperial	American
Onion, chopped	1	1	1
Garlic clove, crushed	1	1	1
Carrot, finely diced	1	1	1
Olive oil	45 ml	3 tbsp	3 tbsp
Paprika	15 ml	1 tbsp	1 tbsp
Can chick peas (garbanzos)	430 g	15¹/₂ oz	1 large can
Passata (sieved tomatoes)	60 ml	4 tbsp	4 tbsp
Tomato purée (paste)	15 ml	1 tbsp	1 tbsp
Dried mixed herbs	2.5 ml	¹/₂ tsp	¹/₂ tsp
Salt and freshly ground black pepper			
Frozen peas	50 g	2 oz	¹/₂ cup
To garnish			
Soured (dairy sour) cream			
Caraway seeds			
Sesame seeds			

1. Fry (sauté) the onion, garlic and carrot in the oil for 2 minutes until softened but not browned.

2. Add the paprika and fry for 1 minute, stirring.

3. Add the contents of can of chick peas (including liquid) and the remaining ingredients.

4. Bring to the boil, reduce the heat and simmer gently for about 10 minutes until thickened.

Serving suggestion

Spoon over portions of any cooked ribbon noodles. Top each with a spoonful of soured cream and a sprinkling of caraway and sesame seeds.

 Preparation time: 5 minutes
Cooking time: 13 minutes

RUSTIC AUBERGINE AND RED KIDNEY BEAN SAUCE

You can substitute other canned pulses for the red kidney beans.

Serves 4	Metric	Imperial	American
Small aubergine (eggplant), diced	1	1	1
Salt			
Olive oil	45 ml	3 tbsp	3 tbsp
Garlic cloves, crushed	1	1	1
Can red kidney beans, drained	430 g	15$^{1}/_{2}$ oz	1 large can
Tomato purée (paste)	30 ml	2 tbsp	2 tbsp
Sun-dried tomato, chopped	1	1	1
Vegetable stock	150 ml	$^{1}/_{4}$ pt	$^{2}/_{3}$ cup
Freshly ground black pepper			
Chopped basil	15 ml	1 tbsp	1 tbsp
To garnish			
Mascarpone cheese			
A few sprigs of basil			

1. Sprinkle the aubergine with salt in a colander and leave to stand for 30 minutes. Rinse thoroughly in cold water and pat dry with kitchen paper.

2. Heat the oil in a saucepan, add the garlic and aubergine and fry (sauté), stirring for 5 minutes.

3. Add the remaining ingredients, except the basil, bring to the boil, reduce the heat and simmer gently for 15 minutes until sauce is reduced and slightly thickened.

4. Stir in the chopped basil.

Serving suggestion

Spoon over portions of cooked spaghetti and garnish each with a spoonful of mascarpone cheese and a sprig of basil.

 Preparation time: 5 minutes plus standing time
Cooking time: 20 minutes

GOLDEN PEPPER WITH AUBERGINE

The yellow (bell) peppers make an interesting colour combination with the aubergines (eggplant), although you can substitute red or orange peppers instead.

Serves 4	Metric	Imperial	American
Large aubergine (eggplant), diced	1	1	1
Salt			
Olive oil	60 ml	4 tbsp	4 tbsp
Red onion, thinly sliced	1	1	1
Garlic clove, crushed	1	1	1
Yellow (bell) pepper, cut in thin strips	1	1	1
Ripe tomatoes, skinned, seeded and chopped	2	2	2
Few drops of anchovy essence (extract)			
Dried oregano	2.5 ml	1/2 tsp	1/2 tsp
Freshly ground black pepper			
Dry white wine	150 ml	1/4 pt	2/3 cup
To garnish			
Olive oil			
A few black olives, stoned (pitted)			

1. Place the aubergine in a colander, sprinkle with salt and leave to stand for 30 minutes. Drain, rinse with cold water and pat dry with kitchen paper.

2. Heat 45 ml/3 tbsp of the oil in a saucepan, add the aubergine and fry (sauté) until golden brown and tender, stirring. Remove from the pan and reserve.

3.   Add the remaining oil and fry the onion and garlic for 2 minutes until slightly softened.

4.   Add the pepper, tomatoes, anchovy essence, oregano and a good grinding of pepper. Return the aubergine to the pan, cover and simmer gently for 10 minutes or until pulpy, stirring occasionally.

5.   Add the wine and simmer uncovered until well reduced – about 5 minutes. Taste and re-season if necessary.

Serving suggestion

Toss cooked spaghetti in a little olive oil. Spoon the sauce over and scatter with a few olives before serving.

 Preparation time: 10 minutes plus standing time
Cooking time: 20 minutes

GREEK MUSHROOM SAUCE

This sauce is equally good chilled and tossed with cold pasta.

Serves 6	Metric	Imperial	American
Onion, chopped	1	1	1
Olive oil	60 ml	4 tbsp	4 tbsp
White wine	300 ml	$^{1}/_{2}$ pt	$1^{1}/_{4}$ cups
Salt and freshly ground black pepper			
Bouquet garni sachet	1	1	1
Garlic clove, finely chopped	1	1	1
Can chopped tomatoes	200 g	7 oz	1 small can
Button mushrooms, quartered	350 g	12 oz	6 cups
To garnish			
Olive oil,	30 ml	2 tbsp	2 tbsp
Chopped parsley			

1. Fry (sauté) the onion in the oil for 3 minutes until softened but not browned.

2. Add the remaining ingredients, bring to the boil, reduce the heat and simmer for about 15 minutes until the mushrooms are cooked and the liquid is reduced and thickened.

3. Remove the bouquet garni sachet, taste the sauce and re-season if necessary.

Serving suggestion
Toss cooked black spaghetti (flavoured with mushrooms) or green tagliatelle (flavoured with spinach) with the olive oil. Spoon the mushroom sauce over and sprinkle with parsley before serving.

 Preparation time: 5 minutes
Cooking time: 20 minutes

DEVILLED MUSHROOM SAUCE

If you like your food very spicy, add extra Tabasco.

Serves 4	Metric	Imperial	American
Onion, finely chopped	1	1	1
Olive oil	30 ml	2 tbsp	2 tbsp
Button mushrooms, quartered	350 g	12 oz	6 cups
Tomatoes, skinned and chopped	2	2	2
Worcestershire sauce	30 ml	2 tbsp	2 tbsp
Tomato ketchup (catsup)	30 ml	2 tbsp	2 tbsp
Few drops of Tabasco sauce			
To garnish			
A knob of unsalted (sweet) butter			
To serve			
Crumbled Wensleydale or Caerphilly cheese			

1. Fry (sauté) the onion in the oil for 2 minutes until softened but not browned.

2. Add the mushrooms and tomatoes and cook, stirring for 2 minutes.

3. Add the remaining ingredients and cook gently for about 5 minutes until mushrooms are cooked but not too soft.

Serving suggestion
Toss cooked spaghetti in a little unsalted butter. Spoon over the sauce and sprinkle with crumbled Wensleydale or Caerphilly cheese.

Preparation time: 5 minutes
Cooking time: 9 minutes

INDONESIAN TOFU WITH MUSHROOMS

Make sure you buy the firm tofu, not the silken smooth variety.

Serves 4	Metric	Imperial	American
Peanut butter	*30 ml*	*2 tbsp*	*2 tbsp*
Clear honey	*15 ml*	*1 tbsp*	*1 tbsp*
Soy sauce	*75 ml*	*5 tbsp*	*5 tbsp*
Red chilli, seeded and chopped	*1*	*1*	*1*
Red wine vinegar	*15 ml*	*1 tbsp*	*1 tbsp*
Tomato juice	*250 ml*	*8 fl oz*	*1 cup*
Tofu, cubed	*285 g*	*10 oz*	*1 packet*
Flat mushrooms, sliced	*175 g*	*6 oz*	*3 cups*
Sunflower oil	*30 ml*	*2 tbsp*	*2 tbsp*
Red (bell) peppers, diced	*2*	*2*	*2*
Beansprouts	*175 g*	*6 oz*	*1¹/₂ cups*
Chopped coriander (cilantro)	*15 ml*	*1 tbsp*	*1 tbsp*

1. Mix the peanut butter with the honey, soy sauce, chilli, vinegar and tomato juice in a saucepan. Heat, stirring, until melted.

2. Remove from the heat and stir in the tofu and mushrooms. Leave to stand for at least 30 minutes.

3. Heat the oil in a large frying pan (skillet) and fry (sauté) the peppers for 2 minutes. Add the beansprouts, coriander and tofu mixture. Cook, stirring over a high heat for 4 minutes.

Serving suggestion
Serve with cooked Chinese egg noodles.

 Preparation time: 10 minutes plus standing time
Cooking time: 8 minutes

CHANTERELLE CREAM RAGÙ

Peeled, sliced field mushrooms are the best alternative to chanterelles for this rich sauce. Accompany with crusty bread and a crisp green salad.

Serves 4	Metric	Imperial	American
Streaky bacon, rinded and diced	*100 g*	*4 oz*	*1 cup*
Butter	*25 g*	*1 oz*	*2 tbsp*
Large onions, halved and sliced	*2*	*2*	*2*
Chanterelles, halved	*450 g*	*1 lb*	*8 cups*
White wine	*150 ml*	*¹/₄ pt*	*²/₃ cup*
Chicken stock	*150 ml*	*¹/₄ pt*	*²/₃ cup*
Soy sauce	*30 ml*	*2 tbsp*	*2 tbsp*
Freshly ground black pepper			
Cornflour (cornstarch)	*15 ml*	*1 tbsp*	*1 tbsp*
Single (light) cream	*120 ml*	*4 fl oz*	*¹/₂ cup*
Chopped coriander (cilantro) or parsley	*30 ml*	*2 tbsp*	*2 tbsp*

1. Fry (sauté) the bacon in the butter for 2 minutes, stirring. Add the onion and cook, stirring for 2 minutes until softened.

2. Add the chanterelles, wine, stock, soy sauce and a good grinding of pepper. Stir well then bring to the boil. Reduce heat and simmer for 10 minutes.

3. Blend the cornflour with the cream. Stir into the mixture, bring to the boil and cook, stirring for 2 minutes.

Serving suggestion
Spoon over cooked rotelli and sprinkle with chopped herbs.

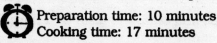 Preparation time: 10 minutes
Cooking time: 17 minutes

Sweet Potato and Cucumber Cheese

You can buy ready-made croûtons as a soup garnish. To make your own, cut sliced bread into very small dice. Fry (sauté) in olive oil until golden. Add a crushed garlic clove or 5 ml/1 tsp dried mixed herbs to the oil for flavour, if liked. Drain on kitchen paper.

Serves 4	Metric	Imperial	American
Large sweet potato, finely diced	1	1	1
Cucumber, diced	1	1	1
Dry white wine	150 ml	1/4 pt	2/3 cup
Milk	300 ml	1/2 pt	1 1/4 cups
Plain (all-purpose) flour	25 g	1 oz	1/4 cup
Butter	25 g	1 oz	2 tbsp
Cheddar cheese, grated	75 g	3 oz	3/4 cup
Salt and white pepper			
Dijon mustard	5 ml	1 tsp	1 tsp
To garnish			
Chopped parsley			

1. Cook sweet potato in boiling water until just tender, about 5 minutes, depending on size of dice. Drain.

2. Simmer the cucumber in the wine for 6-8 minutes until just tender. Lift out cucumber with a draining spoon and add to the potato.

3. Whisk the milk and flour together until smooth. Stir into the wine with the butter and bring to the boil, stirring. Simmer for 2 minutes.

4. Stir in the cheese and season to taste with the salt, pepper and mustard.

5.   Gently stir in the sweet potato and cucumber and heat through until piping hot.

Serving suggestion

Spoon over cooked wholewheat spaghetti and sprinkle with plain, garlic or herb-flavoured croûtons before serving.

 Preparation time: 10 minutes
Cooking time: 15 minutes

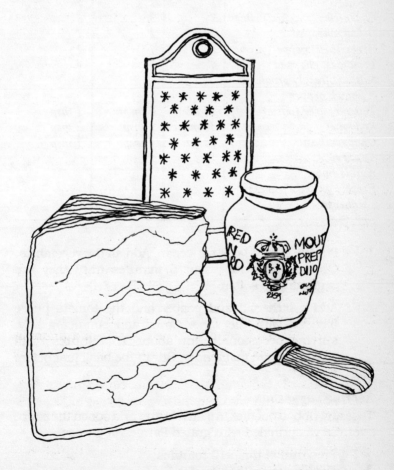

RATATOUILLE

This ever-popular vegetable dish makes a perfect sauce for pasta.

Serves 4-6	Metric	Imperial	American
Olive oil	45 ml	3 tbsp	3 tbsp
Small aubergine (eggplant), diced	1	1	1
Courgettes (zucchini) sliced	3	3	3
Onion, chopped	1	1	1
Green (bell) pepper, diced	1	1	1
Tomatoes, chopped	4	4	4
Salt and freshly ground black pepper			
Tomato purée (paste)	15 ml	1 tbsp	1 tbsp
Red wine	30 ml	2 tbsp	2 tbsp
Chopped basil	15 ml	1 tbsp	1 tbsp
To serve			
A little butter			
Freshly grated Parmesan cheese			

1. Put the oil in a large saucepan. Add all the vegetables. Cook, stirring for about 5 minutes until they are beginning to soften.

2. Add a little salt and pepper and the tomato purée blended with the wine. Cover and simmer gently, stirring occasionally for about 15 minutes until vegetables are just tender. Stir in the basil just before serving.

Serving suggestion
Toss any ribbon noodles in a little butter and spoon the sauce over. Serve sprinkled with grated Parmesan cheese.

Preparation time: 10 minutes
Cooking time: 20 minutes

QUICK CREAMY CORN AND VEGETABLE SAUCE

You only need a few cans and a packet of dried pasta in the cupboard and you can always make a nutritious and filling meal.

Serves 4	Metric	Imperial	American
Can creamed sweetcorn (corn)	300 g	11 oz	1 large can
Can mixed diced vegetables, drained	200 g	7 oz	1 small can
Cheddar cheese, grated	50 g	2 oz	1/2 cup
Dried mixed herbs	2.5 ml	1/2 tsp	1/2 tsp
Freshly ground black pepper			
A little milk			
To garnish			
Crisp, crumbled bacon or chopped parsley			
To serve			
Extra grated Cheddar cheese			

1. Empty the corn into a saucepan. Stir in the drained vegetables, cheese, herbs and a good grinding of pepper. Heat through, stirring all the time until piping hot.

2. Thin slightly with a little milk if liked.

Serving suggestion
Toss with cooked farfalle and sprinkle with crisp crumbled bacon or chopped parsley. Serve with extra grated cheese handed separately.

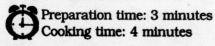

Preparation time: 3 minutes
Cooking time: 4 minutes

GREEN ASPARAGUS HOLLANDAISE SAUCE

When asparagus is out of season, use canned or frozen spears. The texture and flavour won't be quite as good though. Reserve the asparagus trimmings and cooking liquid to make soup.

Serves 4	Metric	Imperial	American
Asparagus	450 g	1 lb	1 lb
Bunch of watercress	1	1	1
Chopped parsley	30 ml	2 tbsp	2 tbsp
Eggs	2	2	2
Lemon juice	30 ml	1 tbsp	1 tbsp
Butter, melted	100 g	4 oz	1/2 cup
Caster (superfine) sugar	1.5 ml	1/4 tsp	1/4 tsp
Salt and white pepper			
To garnish			
Cayenne			

1.   Trim the asparagus stalks and tie spears in a bundle.

2.   Stand the bundle in a pan of boiling, lightly salted water. Cover with a lid or foil and cook for 10 minutes. Turn off heat and leave for 5 minutes. Drain. Cut spears into short lengths.

3.   Meanwhile trim off the watercress stalks and chop the leaves, reserving a few small sprigs for garnish. Mix with the parsley.

4.   Whisk the eggs in a saucepan with the lemon juice. Gradually whisk in the melted butter. Cook, whisking all the time, over a gentle heat until thickened. Do not allow to boil or the mixture will curdle.

5. Add the asparagus and sugar, season to taste and allow to heat through very gently.

Serving suggestion

Add to cooked conchiglie and toss lightly. Garnish with a sprinkling of cayenne and the few reserved watercress sprigs.

Preparation time: 15 minutes
Cooking time: 20 minutes

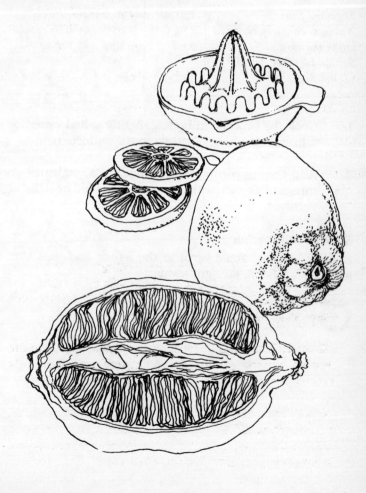

WALNUT AND BROCCOLI SENSATION

Try substituting cauliflower for the broccoli for a change

Serves 4	Metric	Imperial	American
Broccoli, cut into tiny florets	225 g	8 oz	1/2 lb
Mayonnaise	120 ml	4 fl oz	1/2 cup
Fromage frais	120 ml	4 fl oz	1/2 cup
Walnuts, coarsely chopped	25 g	1 oz	1/4 cup
Dijon mustard	5 ml	1 tsp	1 tsp
Salt and freshly ground black pepper			

1. Cook the broccoli in boiling, lightly salted water for 4 minutes. Drain and return to the saucepan.

2. Add the mayonnaise, fromage frais, walnuts and mustard. Season with salt and pepper and heat through gently.

Serving suggestion
Add cooked tagliatelle verdi to the sauce and toss over a gentle heat. Serve straight away.

Preparation time: 5 minutes
Cooking time: 6 minutes

MEDITERRANEAN COURGETTE SAUCE

This is equally good made with diced marrow (squash) instead of courgettes (zucchini).

Serves 4	Metric	Imperial	American
Olive oil	60 ml	4 tbsp	4 tbsp
Onion, chopped	1	1	1
Garlic clove, crushed	1	1	1
Courgettes (zucchini), sliced	6	6	6
Ripe tomatoes, skinned, seeded and chopped	4	4	4
Tomato purée (paste)	15 ml	1 tbsp	1 tbsp
Caster (superfine) sugar	5 ml	1 tsp	1 tsp
Salt and freshly ground black pepper			
Black olives, stoned (pitted)	12	12	12
To garnish			
Extra olive oil			
Freshly grated Parmesan cheese			

1. Heat the oil in a large saucepan. Add the onion and fry (sauté) for 3 minutes until softened but not browned.

2. Add the garlic, courgettes and tomatoes and cook, stirring for 3 minutes until courgettes are slightly softened.

3. Add the tomato purée, sugar, a little salt and pepper and the olives. Cover and simmer gently for 15 minutes.

Serving suggestion
Spoon over cooked linguini, drizzle with a little extra olive oil and serve with lots of grated Parmesan cheese.

 Preparation time: 10 minutes
Cooking time: 21 minutes

SALSA AL POMODORO

This is a basic tomato sauce which can be used on its own or livened up with anything from canned fish to vegetables or pepperoni. Use a can of chopped tomatoes instead of passata (sieved tomatoes) if you prefer a more textured sauce.

Serves 4	Metric	Imperial	American
Olive oil	45 ml	3 tbsp	3 tbsp
Garlic cloves, crushed	2	2	2
Large onion, finely chopped	1	1	1
Carrot, finely diced	1	1	1
Celery stick, finely chopped (optional)	1	1	1
Jar passata (sieved tomatoes)	500 ml	17 fl oz	2¹/₄ cups
Caster (superfine) sugar	5 ml	1 tsp	1 tsp
Chopped basil or marjoram	15 ml	1 tbsp	1 tbsp
Salt and freshly ground black pepper			
To garnish			
Freshly grated Parmesan cheese			

1. Heat the oil in a saucepan. Add the garlic, onion, carrot and celery, if using, and cook gently, stirring for 3 minutes until onion is softened but not browned.

2. Add the passata and sugar, cover and simmer gently for 30 minutes.

3. Stir in the herbs and season to taste with salt and lots of pepper.

Serving suggestion

Add to any cooked pasta, toss well and top with lots of grated
Parmesan cheese.

 Preparation time: 10 minutes
Cooking time: 33 minutes

CRUNCHY CAULIFLOWER WITH CORIANDER SAUCE

The courgettes (zucchini) are added for colour. Use peas or green beans instead if preferred.

Serves 4	Metric	Imperial	American
Butter	*75 g*	*3 oz*	*1/3 cup*
Thick slices bread, cubed	*2*	*2*	*2*
Onion, chopped	*1*	*1*	*1*
Garlic clove, crushed	*1*	*1*	*1*
Ground cumin	*5 ml*	*1 tsp*	*1 tsp*
Courgettes (zucchini), diced	*2*	*2*	*2*
Small cauliflower, cut in tiny florets	*1*	*1*	*1*
Double (heavy) cream	*150 ml*	*1/4 pt*	*2/3 cup*
Chopped coriander (cilantro)	*15 ml*	*1 tbsp*	*1 tbsp*
Salt and freshly ground black pepper			
To garnish			
A few sprigs of coriander (cilantro)			

1. Melt 50 g/2 oz/1/4 cup of the butter in a frying pan (skillet) and fry (sauté) the bread cubes until crisp and golden. Drain on kitchen paper.

2. Melt the remaining butter in a saucepan, add the onion and garlic and fry gently for 2 minutes. Add the cumin and fry for 1 minute.

3. Add the courgettes, stir gently then cover, reduce heat and simmer for 5 minutes until courgettes are just tender.

4. Meanwhile cook the cauliflower florets in boiling salted water for 4-5 minutes until just tender. Drain.

5. Add the cauliflower to the courgette mixture. Stir in the cream, coriander and seasoning. Heat through. Just before serving, stir in the croûtons.

Serving suggestion
Add to cooked rigatoni, toss well and serve garnished with a few sprigs of coriander.

 Preparation time: 10 minutes
Cooking time: 12 minutes

SPICED CARROT AND GARLIC SAUCE

A watercress, orange and tomato salad makes a delicious accompaniment to this dish.

Serves 4	Metric	Imperial	American
Carrots, chopped	750 g	1½ lb	6 cups
Milk	30 ml	2 tbsp	2 tbsp
Butter	40 g	1½ oz	3 tbsp
Garlic clove, crushed	1	1	1
Mixed (apple pie) spice	1.5 ml	¼ tsp	¼ tsp
Salt and freshly ground black pepper			
To garnish			
Chopped parsley			
Crumbled Feta cheese			

1. Put the carrots in a saucepan with just enough water to cover them. Bring to the boil and cook for about 10 minutes until really tender. Drain, but reserve the cooking liquid.

2. Turn the carrots into a food processor or blender with the milk, butter and garlic. Run the machine until the mixture is smooth.

3. Return to the saucepan. Add the mixed spice, salt and pepper to taste and enough of the cooking water to give a smooth purée. Heat through gently until piping hot.

Serving suggestion
Spoon over cooked spaghetti. Sprinkle with parsley and crumbled Feta cheese before serving.

Preparation time: 15 minutes
Cooking time: 12 minutes

CHEESY LEEK SUPPER SAUCE

For extra colour and flavour, try adding a diced green or red (bell) pepper when cooking the leeks.

Serves 4	Metric	Imperial	American
Leeks, sliced	*3*	*3*	*3*
Butter	*50 g*	*2 oz*	*¹/₄ cup*
Plain (all-purpose) flour	*20 g*	*³/₄ oz*	*3 tbsp*
Milk	*300 ml*	*¹/₂ pt*	*1¹/₄ cups*
Dijon mustard	*5 ml*	*1 tsp*	*1 tsp*
Cheddar cheese, grated	*75 g*	*3 oz*	*³/₄ cup*
Salt and freshly ground black pepper			
To garnish			
Chopped parsley			
To serve			
Grated Cheddar cheese			

1. Fry (sauté) the leeks in the butter for 2 minutes until they begin to soften. Reduce heat, cover and cook gently for 10 minutes until tender.

2. Stir in the flour and cook for 1 minute. Gradually blend in the milk. Bring to the boil and simmer for 2 minutes, stirring.

3. Stir in the mustard, cheese and salt and pepper to taste.

Serving suggestion
Add cooked short-cut macaroni. Toss well. Turn into a flameproof dish. Sprinkle with a little more cheese and brown under a hot grill (broiler).

Preparation time: 5 minutes
Cooking time: 10 minutes

Puréed Spinach with Anchovy

When fresh spinach is unavailable, use 225 g/8 oz/1 cup frozen spinach thawed and squeezed out well.

Serves 4	Metric	Imperial	American
Can anchovy fillets	50 g	2 oz	1 small can
Milk	45 ml	3 tbsp	3 tbsp
Spinach	450 g	1 lb	1 lb
Bunch of spring onions (scallions), chopped	1	1	1
Olive oil	45 ml	3 tbsp	3 tbsp
Butter	25 g	1 oz	2 tbsp
Vegetable stock	150 ml	1/4 pt	2/3 cup
Nutmeg	1.5 ml	1/4 tsp	1/4 tsp
Crème fraîche	30 ml	2 tbsp	2 tbsp
Freshly ground black pepper			
To garnish			
Parma ham or thinly sliced Milano salami, cut in thin strips	25 g	1 oz	1/4 cup
To serve			
Grated Pecorino cheese			

1. Soak the anchovies in milk for 5 minutes, drain and chop.

2. Wash the spinach well under running water. Place in a saucepan with any water adhering to the leaves. Cover and cook gently for 4-5 minutes until really tender. Drain well, then squeeze out any remaining moisture.

3. Fry (sauté) the spring onions in the oil and butter for 5 minutes until soft. Add the anchovies and spinach and cook for a further 1 minute.

4.   Place in a blender or processor. Add the stock and run the machine until mixture is smooth. Stir in the nutmeg and crème fraîche and season to taste with pepper.

5.   Return to the saucepan and heat through, stirring until piping hot.

Serving suggestion
Spoon over cooked spaghetti and top with strips of Parma ham or Milano salami. Serve with grated Pecorino cheese.

 Preparation time: 10 minutes
Cooking time: 13 minutes

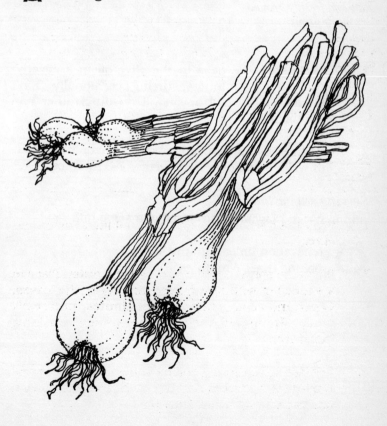

CREAMY PEAS CRÉCY-STYLE

This sauce is also good made with half peas and half young broad (navy) beans.

Serves 4	Metric	Imperial	American
Frozen peas	225 g	8 oz	2 cups
Olive oil	60 ml	4 tbsp	4 tbsp
Bunch of watercress	1	1	1
Chopped basil leaves	30 ml	2 tbsp	2 tbsp
Crème fraîche	120 ml	4 fl oz	¹/₂ cup
Grated nutmeg			
Salt and freshly ground black pepper			

1. Gently stew the peas in the olive oil in a covered saucepan for 4 minutes, stirring occasionally. Don't have the heat too high or you will fry (sauté) rather than stew them.

2. Add the remaining ingredients with seasoning to taste, stir well and simmer for a further 2-3 minutes.

Serving suggestion
Add to cooked tagliarini, toss well and serve hot.

 Preparation time: 5 minutes
Cooking time: 7 minutes

BELGIAN-STYLE PIMIENTO SAUCE

To make chicory less bitter, remove the core by cutting out a 2 cm/³/₄ in cone shape from the base.

Serves 4	Metric	Imperial	American
Olive oil	120 ml	4 fl oz	¹/₂ cup
Bunch of spring onions (scallions), chopped	1	1	1
Heads chicory (Belgian endive), sliced	2	2	2
Can pimiento caps, drained and cut in thin strips	200 g	7 oz	1 small can
Button mushrooms, sliced	50 g	2 oz	1 cup
Garlic clove, crushed	1	1	1
Capers, drained	10 ml	2 tsp	2 tsp
Salt and freshly ground black pepper			
To serve			
Freshly grated Parmesan cheese			

1. Heat half the oil in a saucepan. Add the onions and chicory and cook gently for 3 minutes, stirring.

2. Add the remaining oil and all other ingredients and cook, stirring occasionally for about 5 minutes until chicory is just tender.

Serving suggestion
Add to cooked wholewheat spaghetti, toss well and serve with lots of grated Parmesan cheese.

 Preparation time: 10 minutes
Cooking time: 8 minutes

ROAST VEGETABLE MEDLEY

Try adding a layer of salami slices for the last 10 minutes roasting time.

Serves 4	Metric	Imperial	American
Courgettes (zucchini), cut in chunks	*2*	*2*	*2*
Red onion, quartered	*1*	*1*	*1*
Small aubergine (eggplant), cut in chunks	*1*	*1*	*1*
Yellow, red and green (bell) peppers, each quartered	*1×3*	*1×3*	*1×3*
Olive oil			
Dried oregano	*5 ml*	*1 tsp*	*1 tsp*
Salt and freshly ground black pepper			
To garnish			
Mozzarella, sliced	*225 g*	*8 oz*	*¹/₂ lb*
A few basil leaves, chopped			

1.   Put the prepared vegetables in a roasting tin (pan).

2.   Drizzle with olive oil and sprinkle with the oregano and a little salt and pepper.

3.   Roast in the oven at 190°C/375°F/gas mark 5 for about 30 minutes, stirring once or twice, until turning golden brown on top.

Serving suggestion
Spoon the vegetables and the juices over cooked fettucci in a flameproof dish. Top with mozzarella, grill (broil) until cheese bubbles and sprinkle with chopped basil.

 Preparation time: 10 minutes
Cooking time: 30 minutes

Cheese, Egg & Cream Sauces

The following sauces have cheese, egg or cream – or all three – as their main ingredient. They are quite rich and are good served with a crisp mixed leaf salad and some warm crusty bread – perhaps ciabatta flavoured with olives, mushrooms or sun-dried tomatoes.

TARRAGON PEPPER SAUCE

This sauce not only tastes wonderful with pasta, but it also makes a delicious sauce to serve with grilled steak.

Serves 4	Metric	Imperial	American
Butter	*25 g*	*1 oz*	*2 tbsp*
Small onion, finely chopped	*1*	*1*	*1*
Chopped tarragon	*30 ml*	*2 tbsp*	*2 tbsp*
White wine vinegar	*30 ml*	*2 tbsp*	*2 tbsp*
Dry white wine	*120 ml*	*4 fl oz*	*1/2 cup*
Soft cheese with black pepper	*150 g*	*5 oz*	*1/2 cup*
Single (light) cream	*150 ml*	*1/4 pt*	*2/3 cup*
To garnish			
Pastrami slices, cut in thin strips	*2*	*2*	*2*
A few sprigs of tarragon			

1. Melt the butter in a saucepan. Add the chopped onion and cook gently for 2 minutes until softened but not browned.

2. Add the tarragon, vinegar and wine and boil rapidly until well reduced and thickened.

3. Stir in the cheese and cream and heat through gently for 2-3 minutes.

Serving suggestion
Add to cooked multi-coloured pasta shapes. Toss well and garnish with strips of pastrami and a few sprigs of tarragon.

Preparation time: 5 minutes
Cooking time: 9-10 minutes

FOUR-CHEESE SAUCE

Experiment with different kinds of melting cheese. But remember that if one is too strong, it will swamp the flavour of the rest.

Serves 4	Metric	Imperial	American
Plain (all-purpose) flour	25 g	1 oz	1/4 cup
Milk	600 ml	1 pt	2 1/2 cups
Butter	25 g	1 oz	2 tbsp
Bay leaf	1	1	1
Emmental (Swiss) cheese, grated	50 g	2 oz	1/2 cup
Fontina cheese, chopped	50 g	2 oz	1/2 cup
Mozzarella cheese, grated or chopped	50 g	2 oz	1/2 cup
Freshly grated Pecorino cheese	50 g	2 oz	1/2 cup
To garnish			
Freshly ground black pepper			
Basil leaves, torn into pieces	6	6	6

1. Whisk the flour and milk together in a saucepan until smooth. Add the butter and bay leaf and bring to the boil, whisking all the time until thickened and smooth. Simmer for 2 minutes, stirring.

2. Remove the bay leaf. Stir in the cheeses and heat through until melted.

Serving suggestion

Add to cooked tagliatelle verdi (green tagliatelle) and toss well. Serve with a good grinding of black pepper and the torn basil leaves scattered over.

 Preparation time: 10 minutes
Cooking time: 6 minutes

RICOTTA CHEESE AND BROCCOLI SAUCE

Asparagus spears cut in small pieces make a delicious alternative to broccoli.

Serves 4	Metric	Imperial	American
Broccoli, cut in tiny florets	450 g	1 lb	1 lb
Butter, melted	65 g	2¹/₂ oz	scant ¹/₃ cup
Ricotta cheese	175 g	6 oz	³/₄ cup
Freshly grated Parmesan cheese	50 g	2 oz	¹/₂ cup
Chopped parsley	60 ml	4 tbsp	4 tbsp
Cayenne	1.5 ml	¹/₄ tsp	¹/₄ tsp
Salt and freshly ground black pepper			
To garnish			
A knob of butter			

1. Steam the broccoli or boil in lightly salted water until just tender. Drain.

2. Melt the butter in a saucepan. Add the cheeses and parsley and heat through, stirring. Add the broccoli and heat through. Season to taste with salt and pepper.

Serving suggestion
Toss cooked spaghetti in a knob of butter. Pile the Ricotta sauce on top and serve hot.

Preparation time: 5 minutes
Cooking time: 8 minutes

114

WELSH RAREBIT SAUCE

Use cider or white wine instead of beer, if you prefer.

Serves 4	Metric	Imperial	American
Cheddar cheese, grated	350 g	12 oz	3 cups
Made mustard	10 ml	2 tsp	2 tsp
Light ale	60 ml	4 tbsp	4 tbsp
A little milk			
To garnish			
Snipped chives			
Fried buttered breadcrumbs			

1.   Put all the ingredients in a saucepan and heat through until cheese has melted and mixture is well blended. Add a little milk if the mixture seems too sticky.

Serving suggestion
Add to cooked short-cut macaroni and toss well. Sprinkle liberally with chives and fried buttered breadcrumbs before serving.

Preparation time: 5 minutes
Cooking time: 4 minutes

DOLCELATTE CREAM

Ring the changes with other soft blue cheeses.

Serves 4	Metric	Imperial	American
Celery sticks, finely chopped	2	2	2
Butter	25 g	1 oz	2 tbsp
Dolcelatte, diced	100 g	4 oz	1 cup
Medium fat soft cheese	50 g	2 oz	1/4 cup
Single (light) cream	90 ml	6 tbsp	6 tbsp
Chopped parsley	15 ml	1 tbsp	1 tbsp
Freshly ground black pepper			

1. Put celery and butter in a double saucepan or in a bowl over a pan of gently simmering water. Cover and cook gently for about 8 minutes or until softened.

2. Add the cheeses and cook, stirring until smooth and melted.

3. Stir in the cream and parsley. Add plenty of pepper and stir well.

Serving suggestion
Add to cooked tagliatelle verdi (green tagliatelle), toss well and serve piping hot.

Preparation time: 3 minutes
Cooking time: 10 minutes

GARLIC AND HERB CHEESE SAUCE

This is particularly good served as a starter or as a side dish to grilled meat, poultry or fish.

Serves 4-6	Metric	Imperial	American
Cornflour (cornstarch)	15 ml	1 tbsp	1 tbsp
Milk	300 ml	1/2 pt	1 1/4 cups
Butter	15 g	1/2 oz	1 tbsp
Garlic and herb cheese	80 g	3 1/2 oz	3 1/2 oz
Salt and freshly ground black pepper			
To garnish			
Snipped chives			

1. Whisk the cornflour with a little of the milk in a saucepan. Stir in the remaining milk and add the butter.

2. Bring to the boil, stirring until thickened.

3. Add the cheese and stir over a gentle heat until smooth. Season with salt and pepper.

Serving suggestion
Add to multi-coloured pasta shapes. Toss and sprinkle with snipped chives before serving.

Preparation time: 3 minutes
Cooking time: 4 minutes

GOATHERD'S MOUNTAIN SPECIAL

The crumbled goat's cheese is added just before serving so it only just begins to melt as it is served.

Serves 4-6	Metric	Imperial	American
Olive oil	120 ml	4 fl oz	¹/₂ cup
Garlic cloves, crushed	2	2	2
Ripe tomatoes, diced	4	4	4
Salt and freshly ground black pepper			
Basil leaves, torn in pieces	16	16	16
Goat's cheese, roughly crumbled	50 g	2 oz	¹/₂ cup
To garnish			
A few black olives, stoned (pitted) (optional)			

1. Heat the oil in a saucepan. Add the garlic and cook gently for 1 minute.

2. Add the tomatoes and a little salt and pepper and cook gently for 1-2 minutes, stirring until heated through but with tomatoes still in pieces.

3. Add the basil leaves and toss gently. When ready to serve, add the cheese.

Serving suggestion
Add cooked spaghettini to the tomato and basil mixture. Toss well. Add the cheese and toss again. Pile onto plates and serve immediately garnished with a few black olives if liked.

 Preparation time: 5 minutes
Cooking time: 3 minutes

GOAT'S CHEESE WITH RADICCHIO AND GREEN PEPPERCORN SAUCE

This is particularly good served with a tomato and spring onion (scallion) salad.

Serves 4	Metric	Imperial	American
Butter	25 g	1 oz	2 tbsp
Garlic cloves, finely chopped	2	2	2
Head of radicchio, coarsely shredded	1	1	1
Salt			
Pickled green peppercorns	5 ml	1 tsp	1 tsp
Double (heavy) cream	250 ml	8 fl oz	1 cup
Goat's cheese, crumbled	50 g	2 oz	¹/₂ cup
To garnish			
Freshly ground black or green pepper			

1. Melt the butter in a saucepan. Add the garlic and radicchio, toss then cover and cook gently for 4 minutes.

2. Season lightly with salt and add the peppercorns.

3. In a separate pan, heat the cream. Add half the cheese and whisk until smooth.

4. Stir in the radicchio mixture.

Serving suggestion
Add to cooked farfalle with the remaining cheese. Toss quickly and serve garnished with a good grinding of black or green pepper.

 Preparation time: 5 minutes
Cooking time: 5 minutes

NUTTY GORGONZOLA

This is very rich, so serve in small portions with a crisp salad and some crusty bread.

Serves 6	Metric	Imperial	American
Garlic cloves, finely chopped	*2*	*2*	*2*
Butter	*25 g*	*1 oz*	*2 tbsp*
Gorgonzola, crumbled	*225 g*	*8 oz*	*2 cups*
Walnuts, chopped	*50 g*	*2 oz*	*1/2 cup*
Salt and freshly ground black pepper			
Milk or single (light) cream	*30 ml*	*2 tbsp*	*2 tbsp*
Freshly grated Parmesan cheese	*30 ml*	*2 tbsp*	*2 tbsp*
To garnish			
Chopped parsley			

1. Cook the garlic gently in the butter for 1 minute.

2. Add the remaining ingredients and heat through gently until the cheese is melted and well combined. Do not allow to boil.

Serving suggestion
Add to cooked wholewheat spaghetti, toss well and serve garnished with parsley.

Preparation time: 5 minutes
Cooking time: 3 minutes

MIDDLE EASTERN COTTAGE CHEESE
SAUCE

This dish needs to be served with a good mixed salad dressed with olive oil and red wine vinegar.

Serves 4-6	Metric	Imperial	American
Cottage cheese	900 g	2 lb	4 cups
Caraway seeds	50 g	2 oz	1/2 cup
Poppy seeds	50 g	2 oz	1/2 cup
Freshly ground black pepper			
To garnish			
Knob of butter			
Coarse sea salt	5 ml	1 tsp	1 tsp
Paprika			

1. Mix the cottage cheese, seeds and a good grinding of pepper together. Place in a bowl over a pan of hot water (or in a double saucepan) and warm gently but do not allow to boil.

Serving suggestion

Toss any wide ribbon noodles in the butter. Pile the warm cheese mixture on top and sprinkle with coarse sea salt and paprika before serving.

Preparation time: 3 minutes
Cooking time: 3 minutes

ATHENIAN SAUCE

This is a glorious mixture of salty and sweet flavours. It makes a delicious summer lunch dish. Once cooked, serve immediately before the cheese melts completely.

Serves 4	Metric	Imperial	American
Olive oil	60 ml	4 tbsp	4 tbsp
Garlic cloves, chopped	2	2	2
Spring onions (scallions), chopped	4	4	4
Dried oregano	5 ml	1 tsp	1 tsp
Large beefsteak tomato, diced	1	1	1
Freshly ground black pepper			
Black Greek olives, stoned (pitted)	75 g	3 oz	1/2 cup
Freshly grated Parmesan cheese	30 ml	2 tbsp	2 tbsp
Chilled Feta cheese, crumbled	100 g	4 oz	1 cup
Roughly chopped mint	30 ml	2 tbsp	2 tbsp
To serve			
A little extra olive oil			
Freshly grated Parmesan cheese			

1. Heat the oil in a saucepan. Add the garlic and spring onions and soften for 1 minute.

2. Add the oregano, tomato and a good grinding of pepper and cook gently for 1-2 minutes until hot but tomatoes still hold their shape.

3. Add the remaining ingredients and toss lightly over a gentle heat to combine.

Serving suggestion

Toss cooked spaghetti in a little olive oil. Add the Feta mixture, toss quickly and serve straight away with grated Parmesan cheese handed separately.

 Preparation time: 5 minutes
Cooking time: 4 minutes

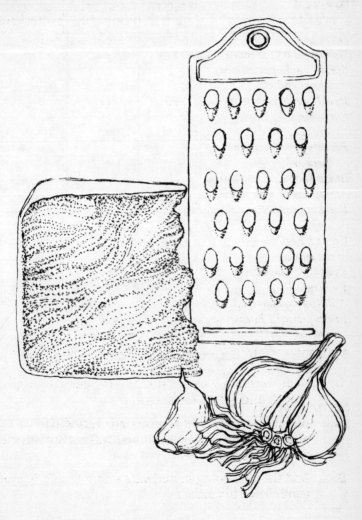

FRESH PARMESAN WITH AVOCADO CREAM

This sauce is particularly good served over tortellini, stuffed with mushrooms as well as the suggestion given below.

Serves 4	Metric	Imperial	American
Double (heavy) cream	175 ml	6 fl oz	³/₄ cup
Ripe avocado peeled and stoned (pitted)	1	1	1
Freshly grated Parmesan cheese	75 g	3 oz	³/₄ cup
Lemon juice	30 ml	2 tbsp	2 tbsp
Salt and freshly ground black pepper			
To garnish			
Tiny sprigs of watercress			

1. Place the cream in a saucepan and heat gently but do not boil.

2. Meanwhile purée the avocado in a blender or food processor with the cheese and lemon juice. Alternatively, mash well with a fork then beat until smooth.

3. Stir into the hot cream and season well. Heat gently for a further 2-3 minutes. Use immediately.

Serving suggestion
Pour over cooked tagliatelle al pomodoro (red tagliatelle) or a mixture of red and green (tagliatelle verdi). Garnish with a few tiny sprigs of watercress scattered over.

 Preparation time: 5 minutes
Cooking time: 4 minutes

TOCCO DI NOCCI

This walnut and mascarpone cheese sauce is also good served with stuffed pasta shapes.

Serves 4	Metric	Imperial	American
Shelled walnuts	225 g	8 oz	2 cups
Thick slice of white bread, crusts removed	1	1	1
Milk	75 ml	5 tbsp	5 tbsp
Garlic clove, crushed	1	1	1
Salt and freshly ground black pepper			
Olive oil	45 ml	3 tbsp	3 tbsp
Mascarpone cheese	100 g	4 oz	1/2 cup

1. Place the nuts in boiling water for 2 minutes. Drain and rub off the skins in a clean tea towel (dish cloth).

2. Soak the bread in the milk.

3. Grind the nuts to a fine powder in a blender or food processor.

4. Squeeze out the bread and add to the nuts with the garlic and a little salt and pepper. Run the machine until mixture is smooth.

5. With the machine running, add the oil in a thin stream and then finally add the cheese.

Serving suggestion
Add to freshly cooked tagliatelle and toss over a gentle heat until hot through. Serve immediately.

 Preparation time: 10-15 minutes

COTTAGE CHEESE AND PINE NUT SAUCE

Try this sauce cold with any cooked pasta shells too.

Serves 4	Metric	Imperial	American
Olive oil	60 ml	4 tbsp	4 tbsp
Red (bell) pepper, chopped	1	1	1
Green (bell) pepper, chopped	1	1	1
Spring onions, (scallions), chopped	4	4	4
Pine nuts, roughly crushed	100 g	4 oz	1 cup
Cottage cheese	450 g	1 lb	2 cups
Salt and freshly ground black pepper			
To garnish			
A little extra olive oil			
Twists of lemon			
Cress			

1. Heat the oil in a saucepan. Add the peppers and spring onions and cook gently for 2 minutes.

2. Add the remaining ingredients and cook gently until heated through, stirring all the time.

Serving suggestion
Toss cooked tagliatelle verdi (green tagliatelle) in a little olive oil. Divide between serving plates. Spoon the cheese mixture over and garnish each with a twist of lemon and a little cress.

 Preparation time: 10 minutes
Cooking time: 5 minutes

BASIC CHEESE SAUCE

This can be used as below or as the top layer for lasagne or to coat stuffed cannelloni.

Serves 4	Metric	Imperial	American
Plain (all-purpose) flour	20 g	3/4 oz	3 tbsp
Milk	300 ml	1/2 pt	1¼ cups
Butter	20 g	3/4 oz	1½ tbsp
Bay leaf	1	1	1
Dijon or made English mustard	5 ml	1 tsp	1 tsp
Cheddar cheese, grated	75 g	3 oz	3/4 cup
Salt and freshly ground black pepper			
To garnish			
A little extra grated cheese			

1. Whisk the flour with a little of the milk in a saucepan until smooth. Whisk in the remaining milk and add the butter and bay leaf.

2. Bring to the boil and cook for 2 minutes, stirring all the time.

3. Stir in the mustard and cheese and season to taste with salt and pepper. Discard the bay leaf before use.

Serving suggestion
Add to cooked short-cut macaroni. Toss well and turn into a flameproof serving dish. Top with a little extra grated cheese and brown under a hot grill (broiler).

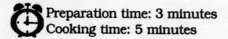 Preparation time: 3 minutes
Cooking time: 5 minutes

JALAPENO PEPPER CREAM

Serve this with an avocado and cucumber salad.

Serves 4-6	Metric	Imperial	American
White wine vinegar	120 ml	4 fl oz	¹/₂ cup
Salt	2.5 ml	¹/₂ tsp	¹/₂ tsp
Small onion, finely chopped	1	1	1
Jalapeno pepper, seeded and chopped	1	1	1
Double (heavy) cream	600 ml	1 pt	2¹/₂ cups
Chopped coriander (cilantro)	30 ml	2 tbsp	2 tbsp

1. Put the vinegar, salt, onion and chilli in a saucepan. Bring to the boil and boil rapidly for about 5 minutes until the mixture is reduced by half.

2. Add the cream, bring to the boil and boil rapidly until the mixture is well reduced and thickened – about 15 minutes.

3. Add half the coriander and stir well.

Serving suggestion
Pour over cooked fettuccine, toss well and sprinkle with the remaining coriander.

Preparation time: 5 minutes
Cooking time: 20 minutes

SALSA ALFREDO

This is one of the simplest ways of serving good fresh pasta – ideal if you've bothered to make your own.

Serves 4	Metric	Imperial	American
Double (heavy) cream	*450 ml*	*³/₄ pt*	*2 cups*
Butter	*50 g*	*2 oz*	*¹/₄ cup*
Freshly grated Parmesan cheese	*175 g*	*6 oz*	*1¹/₂ cups*
Freshly ground black pepper			
To garnish			
Crisp, crumbled bacon (optional)			

1.   Bring the cream and butter to the boil in a saucepan. Reduce the heat and simmer for 1 minute.

2.   Add half the cheese and some pepper and whisk until smooth.

Serving suggestion
Add cooked home-made fettuccine and the rest of the cheese and toss well over a gentle heat. Pile onto warm plates and sprinkle with a good grinding of black pepper and crisp crumbled bacon, if liked.

 Preparation time: 3 minutes
Cooking time: 3 minutes

Salsa alla Carbonara

This sauce is also very good with the addition of 50 g/2 oz/ 1 cup sliced button mushrooms.

Serves 4	Metric	Imperial	American
Unsmoked streaky bacon, cut in small dice	*100 g*	*4 oz*	*³/₄ cup*
Butter	*75 g*	*3 oz*	*¹/₃ cup*
Eggs	*5*	*5*	*5*
Chopped parsley	*30 ml*	*2 tbsp*	*2 tbsp*
Salt and freshly ground black pepper			
Freshly grated Parmesan cheese	*50 g*	*2 oz*	*¹/₂ cup*

1. Fry (sauté) the bacon in the butter until browned.

2. Beat the eggs with the parsley, a little salt and lots of pepper and the cheese.

Serving suggestion
Cook spaghetti in the normal way. Drain and return to the saucepan over a gentle heat. Add the hot bacon in its fat and toss. Add the egg mixture and toss quickly until the spaghetti is coated but do not let it scramble. The mixture should be creamy and hot. Serve straight away.

 Preparation time: 5 minutes
Cooking time: 5 minutes

SALSA ALLA PANNA

For a more exotic version, use Pancetta or a raw cured ham like Parma instead of cooked ham.

Serves 4	Metric	Imperial	American
Butter	*40 g*	*1¹/₂ oz*	*3 tbsp*
Cooked sliced ham, cut in tiny strips	*100 g*	*4 oz*	*1 cup*
Double (heavy) cream	*75 ml*	*5 tbsp*	*5 tbsp*
Salt and freshly ground black pepper			
Freshly grated nutmeg			
To garnish			
Freshly grated Parmesan cheese			

1. Melt the butter in a saucepan (you can use the one you've just used to cook the pasta to save washing up).

2. Add the cream, ham, a sprinkling of salt, a good grinding of pepper and lots of grated nutmeg and heat through for 1 minute.

Serving suggestion

Add cooked mafalde and toss over a gentle heat for 2 minutes. Serve garnished with lots of freshly grated Parmesan cheese.

Preparation time: 5 minutes
Cooking time: 4 minutes

SCRAMBLED EGG AND SMOKED SALMON SAUCE

The trick is to only half-scramble the eggs before adding the pasta so every strand gets bathed in sauce.

Serves 4-6	Metric	Imperial	American
Butter	*15 g*	*¹/₂ oz*	*1 tbsp*
Eggs, beaten	*4*	*4*	*4*
Single (light) cream	*150 ml*	*¹/₄ pt*	*²/₃ cup*
Smoked salmon pieces,			
* cut in tiny strips*	*100 g*	*4 oz*	*1 cup*
Freshly ground black			
* pepper*			
To garnish			
Chopped parsley			

1. Melt the butter in a saucepan. Add the eggs and cream and whisk lightly.

2. Stir over a gentle heat until half scrambled but still quite runny. Stir in the salmon and a good grinding of black pepper.

Serving suggestion

Have spaghetti or bucatini ready, just cooked. Drain and add to the egg mixture and toss lightly over a gentle heat until mixture is just scrambled but still creamy. Serve straight away garnished with chopped parsley.

Preparation time: 5 minutes
Cooking time: 5 minutes

BUTTERS PASTES & SALAD DRESSINGS

The butters and pastes are usually added to hot cooked pasta and the dressings to cold cooked pasta; they are then tossed well to allow the delicious flavours to coat every piece or strand of the pasta. All the pastes can be made in advance and stored in a screw-topped jar in the fridge for up to a week.

BLACK BUTTER

This simple sauce has a wonderfully nutty flavour. It is also delicious served over any stuffed pasta.

Serves 4-6	Metric	Imperial	American
Unsalted (sweet) butter	175 g	6 oz	³/₄ cup
Garlic cloves, finely chopped	3	3	3
Freshly grated Parmesan cheese	175 g	6 oz	1¹/₂ cups
Salt and freshly ground black pepper			
To garnish			
Chopped parsley			

1. Put the butter in a frying pan (skillet) and melt over a moderate heat.

2. When the butter starts to foam, add the garlic and continue cooking until the butter begins to turn brown – about 1 minute. Immediately remove from the heat – do not overcook or it will burn. Stir in the Parmesan, a little salt and lots of black pepper. Either use immediately or cool and store in the fridge until required.

Serving suggestion
Add to hot cooked linguini, toss well over a gentle heat and serve straight away garnished with parsley.

 Preparation time: 3 minutes
Cooking time: 3 minutes

TARRAGON AND GARLIC BUTTER

This mixture is also good spread on slices of French bread, re-shaped into a loaf, wrapped in foil and baked in a moderate oven for about 20 minutes.

Serves 4	Metric	Imperial	American
Butter, softened	*100 g*	*4 oz*	*¹/₂ cup*
Chopped tarragon	*30 ml*	*2 tbsp*	*2 tbsp*
Garlic clove, crushed	*1*	*1*	*1*
Freshly ground black pepper			
To garnish			
Olive oil			
Thin slivers of fresh Parmesan cheese			

1. Mash the butter with the tarragon, garlic and a good grinding of pepper until well blended. Shape into a roll on a sheet of greaseproof (waxed) paper or cling film (plastic wrap). Roll up and chill until required.

Serving suggestion

Either unwrap the butter and cut in thin slices. Toss cooked vermicelli in a little olive oil then pile on plates and dot all over with the slices of tarragon butter and garnish with the slivers of Parmesan. Alternatively, roughly cut up the butter, add to cooked vermicelli or 'angel hair', toss over a gentle heat until melted. Pile onto warm plates and drizzle with olive oil then top with the flakes of Parmesan.

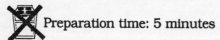 Preparation time: 5 minutes

BAGNA CAUDA

This delicious concoction comes from the Piedmont region of Italy. Sometimes it is flavoured with white truffles, sometimes with walnut oil. It is often served like a fondue in the middle of the table with a selection of vegetables to dip in. It also makes a sensational dressing for pasta.

Serves 4-6	Metric	Imperial	American
Walnut oil	75 ml	5 tbsp	5 tbsp
Olive oil	75 ml	5 tbsp	5 tbsp
Garlic cloves, finely chopped	3	3	3
Can anchovy fillets, drained and chopped	50 g	2 oz	1 small can
Unsalted (sweet) butter	25 g	1 oz	2 tbsp
Tomato, seeded and chopped	1	1	1
Double (heavy) cream (optional)	45 ml	3 tbsp	3 tbsp
Salt			

1. Heat the oil in a saucepan. Add the garlic and fry (sauté) until golden.

2. Reduce the heat, add the anchovies and cook gently, stirring until they have 'melted' into the oil.

3. Stir in the butter until melted. Add the tomato and cream, if using, and heat through. Taste and add salt if necessary.

Serving suggestion
Add to cooked wholewheat spaghetti. Toss well and serve piping hot.

 Preparation time: 5 minutes
Cooking time: 6 minutes

OIL WITH GINGER AND GARLIC

Fresh root ginger (ginger root) is a popular flavouring in Umbria, central Italy. This flavoured oil can either be used straight away or poured into a screw-topped jar and kept for up to 3 weeks in the fridge. Re-heat before pouring over pasta.

Serves 4-6	Metric	Imperial	American
Olive oil	375 ml	13 fl oz	1½ cups
Garlic cloves, chopped	10	10	10
Fresh root ginger (ginger root), grated	45 ml	3 tbsp	3 tbsp
To garnish			
Freshly grated Parmesan cheese			

1. Heat the oil in a saucepan. Add the garlic and ginger and cook for 2-3 minutes until lightly golden.

2. Remove from the heat and either use straight away or cool slightly and store as above.

Serving suggestion
Serve drizzled over 'angel hair', vermicelli or spaghettini with lots of freshly grated Parmesan cheese.

Preparation time: 5 minutes
Cooking time: 4 minutes

PESTO ALLA GENOVESE

This classic paste is one of the highlights of Italian pasta cooking. Don't be tempted to try and use dried basil – it simply won't work.

Serves 4	Metric	Imperial	American
Large basil leaves	14	14	14
Garlic cloves, chopped	2	2	2
Coarse sea salt	5 ml	1 tsp	1 tsp
Pine nuts, toasted	15 ml	1 tbsp	1 tbsp
Freshly grated Parmesan cheese	30 ml	2 tbsp	2 tbsp
Olive oil	45 ml	3 tbsp	3 tbsp
Freshly ground black pepper			
To garnish			
Flakes of butter			
Extra freshly grated Parmesan cheese			

1. Place the basil leaves in a blender or food processor with the garlic and salt and run the machine until they form a purée. Alternatively, you can pound the ingredients in a pestle and mortar.

2. Add the nuts and cheese and blend until smooth, scraping mixture from the sides as necessary.

3. Gradually add the oil a drop at a time until the mixture becomes a thick green sauce. Add a good grinding of pepper.

Serving suggestion

Add to cooked spaghetti or tagliatelle. Toss well over a gentle heat and dot with flakes of butter before serving with more freshly grated Parmesan to sprinkle over.

 Preparation time: 8-10 minutes

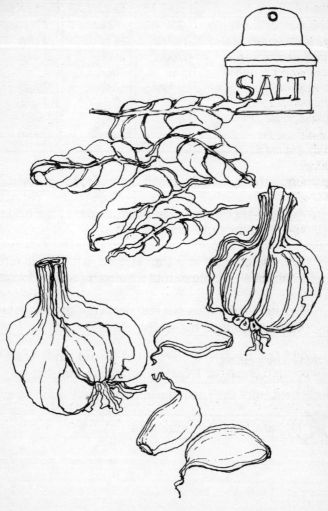

Spinach and Cashew Nut Paste

Another gloriously green paste but with a more subtle flavour than Pesto.

Serves 4-6	Metric	Imperial	American
Young spinach leaves	350 g	12 oz	1½ cups
Grated Pecorino cheese	100 g	4 oz	1 cup
Shelled cashew nuts	100 g	4 oz	1 cup
Garlic cloves, crushed	2	2	2
Lemon juice	30 ml	2 tbsp	2 tbsp
Olive oil	250 ml	8 fl oz	1 cup
Salt and freshly ground black pepper			

1. Chop the spinach in a blender or food processor.

2. Add the cheese, nuts, garlic and lemon juice and run the machine until well blended.

3. Add the olive oil in a thin stream, with the machine running all the time until a smooth paste is formed.

4. Season lightly with salt and pepper. If the sauce is too thick add a little hot water.

Serving suggestion
Add to cooked wholewheat spaghetti and toss well over a gentle heat until the paste has melted. Serve straight away.

Preparation time: 5 minutes

ALMOND AND HERB PASTE

This is an anglicised version of Pesto alla Genovese, but it has an equally fragrant aroma and tempting flavour.

Serves 4	Metric	Imperial	American
Butter	*100 g*	*4 oz*	*¹/₂ cup*
Ground almonds	*50 g*	*2 oz*	*¹/₂ cup*
Freshly grated Parmesan cheese	*20 ml*	*4 tsp*	*4 tsp*
Chopped parsley	*45 ml*	*3 tbsp*	*3 tbsp*
Snipped chives	*15 ml*	*1 tbsp*	*1 tbsp*
Chopped sage	*10 ml*	*2 tsp*	*2 tsp*
Salt and freshly ground black pepper			
To garnish			
Extra freshly grated Parmesan cheese			
Toasted flaked almonds			

1. Mash the butter with the ground almonds.

2. Work in the cheese and herbs and season well.

Serving suggestion
Add to cooked spaghettini and toss well over a gentle heat until the paste has melted and coats all the strands of pasta. Pile onto plates and garnish with extra freshly grated Parmesan and a sprinkling of toasted flaked almonds.

 Preparation time: 8 minutes

SUN-DRIED TOMATO PASTE

Sun-dried tomatoes in olive oil are now readily available in most supermarkets. They are often found along with other Italian antipastos.

Serves 4-6	Metric	Imperial	American
Sun-dried tomatoes, drained, reserving the oil	350 g	12 oz	3 cups
Olive oil			
Freshly grated Parmesan cheese	150 g	5 oz	1^1/4 cups
Chopped mixed nuts	75 g	3 oz	^{3}/4 cup
Chopped parsley	45 ml	3 tbsp	3 tbsp
Garlic cloves	3	3	3

1. Put the tomatoes in a blender or food processor.

2. Make up the reserved tomato oil to 375 ml/13 fl oz/ 1^1/2 cups with olive oil.

3. Add the oil to the blender with the remaining ingredients. Run the machine until the mixture forms a smooth paste, stopping the machine and scraping down the sides from time to time.

4. If the paste is too thick, add a little hot water.

Serving suggestion
Add to any cooked ribbon noodles, toss well over a gentle heat and serve piping hot.

 Preparation time: 5 minutes

COARSE SUN-DRIED TOMATO AND BASIL PASTE

Serve this dish with lots of olive ciabatta bread and a crisp green salad to make this into a memorable meal.

Serves 4-6	Metric	Imperial	American
Garlic cloves	3	3	3
Olive oil	50 ml	2 fl oz	3¹/₂ tbsp
Sun-dried tomato oil	30 ml	2 tbsp	2 tbsp
Freshly grated Parmesan cheese	25 g	1 oz	¹/₄ cup
Basil leaves	8	8	8
Sun-dried tomatoes	200 g	7 oz	1³/₄ cups
Freshly ground black pepper			
To garnish			
Extra freshly grated Parmesan cheese			
A few torn basil leaves			

1. Put the garlic in a blender or processor and chop. Add the olive and tomato oils and run the machine until well blended.

2. Add the cheese and blend briefly again.

3. Add the basil and tomatoes and run the machine until roughly chopped but not a paste. Season with lots of black pepper.

Serving suggestion
Add to cooked spaghetti or bucatini. Toss over a gentle heat, pile onto plates and garnish with extra cheese and a few torn basil leaves.

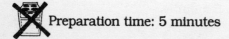 Preparation time: 5 minutes

PIMIENTO AND OLIVE PASTE

Made mainly from store–cupboard ingredients, this paste is ideal for an impromptu supper party. A good tip is to keep a bag of parsley in the freezer. The flavour is just as good as when the leaves are fresh.

Serves 4-6	Metric	Imperial	American
Can pimientos, drained	400 g	14 oz	1 large can
Garlic cloves	2	2	2
Olive oil	300 ml	1/2 pt	1 1/4 cups
Stuffed olives	75 g	3 oz	3/4 cup
Freshly grated Parmesan cheese	50 g	2 oz	1/2 cup
Chopped parsley	60 ml	4 tbsp	4 tbsp
Lemon juice	30 ml	2 tbsp	2 tbsp
Salt and freshly ground black pepper			
To garnish			
Grated Mozzarella cheese			

1. Put all the ingredients except salt and pepper in a food processor or blender.

2. Run the machine until the mixture forms a paste. Stop the machine and scrape down the sides from time to time.

3. Taste and season with a little salt and lots of black pepper.

Serving suggestion
Add to cooked fusilli, toss well over a gentle heat and top with a little grated Mozzarella. Serve straight away.

 Preparation time: 5 minutes

TAPENADE

This is a famous paste from Provence. It is delicious as a pasta dressing or spread on slices of crusty French bread.

Serves 4-6	Metric	Imperial	American
Olive oil	250 ml	8 fl oz	1 cup
Black olives, stoned (pitted)	225 g	8 oz	1¹/₃ cups
Green olives, stoned (pitted)	225 g	8 oz	1¹/₃ cups
Garlic cloves	3	3	3
Parsley	75 g	3 oz	³/₄ cup
Cans anchovies, drained	2 × 50 g	2 × 2 oz	2 small cans
Capers, drained	60 ml	4 tbsp	4 tbsp
Lemon juice	45 ml	3 tbsp	3 tbsp
Freshly ground black pepper			
To garnish			
Fresh Parmesan cheese, cut in thin shavings			

1. Put all the ingredients including a good grinding of pepper in a food processor or blender.

2. Run the machine until a smooth paste is formed. Stop the machine and scrape down the sides from time to time.

Serving suggestion
Add to cooked linguini, toss well over a gentle heat and serve garnished with thin shavings of fresh Parmesan.

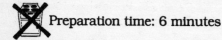 Preparation time: 6 minutes

JAPANESE NOODLE DIPPING SAUCE

To give this a really authentic Japanese flavour, you need to use dashi – a stock made from seaweed – and dried bonito fish flakes. These ingredients are available from Asian food shops. You can improvise using fish stock and 15-30 ml/1-2 tbsp anchovy essence (extract), but the flavour will not be so good.

Serves 4-6	Metric	Imperial	American
Dashi	450 ml	$^3/_4$ pt	2 cups
Mirin (Japanese rice wine)			
or dry sherry	45 ml	3 tbsp	3 tbsp
Soy sauce	45 ml	3 tbsp	3 tbsp
Dried bonito flakes	225 g	8 oz	$^1/_2$ lb

1. Place all the ingredients in a saucepan. Bring slowly to the boil.

2. Reduce the heat and simmer gently for 10 minutes.

3. Strain through a sieve (strainer) lined with muslin (cheesecloth).

Serving suggestion
Pour into 4 or 6 individual bowls. Serve with Japanese soba or somen noodles, either warm or cold and literally dip the noodles into the sauce before eating.

Preparation time: 5 minutes
Cooking time: 10 minutes

GREEN BEAN AND PEANUT DRESSING

This has a wonderful oriental flavour. The serving suggestion below is for Chinese or Japanese noodles, but you could serve it with cold cooked elbow macaroni or spiralli instead.

Serves 4-6	Metric	Imperial	American
Thin green beans, topped, tailed and cut into 2.5 cm/1 in lengths	225 g	8 oz	2 cups
Peanut butter	90 ml	6 tbsp	6 tbsp
Caster (superfine) sugar	30 ml	2 tbsp	2 tbsp
Dashi (available from Asian food shops) or vegetable stock	150 ml	1/4 pt	2/3 cup
Soy sauce	30 ml	2 tbsp	2 tbsp

1. Cook the beans in boiling, salted water for 5 minutes until just tender. Drain, rinse with cold water and drain again.

2. Blend the peanut butter, sugar, stock and soy sauce together in a bowl. Add the beans.

Serving suggestion
Add to cold cooked soba or Chinese egg noodles. Toss well and serve straight away.

Preparation time: 15 minutes, including cooking the beans

TV Supper Dressing

This makes a highly nutritious supper dish, ideal for eating with a fork while watching television!

Serves 4	Metric	Imperial	American
Tomatoes, chopped	4	4	4
Cucumber, diced	1/4	1/4	1/4
Cheddar cheese, cubed	175 g	6 oz	1 1/2 cups
Can sweetcorn (corn), drained	350 g	12 oz	1 large can
Olive oil	45 ml	3 tbsp	3 tbsp
Lemon juice	15 ml	1 tbsp	1 tbsp
Dijon mustard	5 ml	1 tsp	1 tsp
Salt	1.5 ml	1/4 tsp	1/4 tsp
Freshly ground black pepper			

1. Put the tomatoes, cucumber and cheese in a bowl with the sweetcorn and mix gently.

2. Whisk the remaining ingredients together and pour over. Toss lightly.

Serving suggestion
Spoon over cold cooked ruote, toss lightly and add an extra grinding of black pepper. Chill, if liked, before serving.

 Preparation time: 8 minutes

MOZZARELLA AND CHERRY TOMATO VINAIGRETTE

Clean tasting and refreshing – one of the tastiest summer lunch dishes imaginable.

Serves 4	Metric	Imperial	American
Mozzarella, cut in small dice	225 g	8 oz	2 cups
Cherry tomatoes, quartered	350 g	12 oz	3 cups
Basil leaves, torn	16	16	16
Olive oil	250 ml	8 fl oz	1 cup
Red wine vinegar	30 ml	2 tbsp	2 tbsp
Freshly ground black pepper			
To garnish			
A little coarse sea salt			

1. Put all the ingredients, including lots of black pepper in a bowl. Toss lightly and chill for 30 minutes.

Serving suggestion

Add to cold cooked rigatoni. Toss lightly but thoroughly. Serve sprinkled with a little coarse sea salt.

 Preparation time: 8 minutes, plus chilling time

PROVENÇE-STYLE DRESSING

This is a bit like a Salade Niçoise, but using pasta instead of potatoes.

Serves 4	Metric	Imperial	American
French beans, topped, tailed and cut in three	*225 g*	*8 oz*	*2 cups*
Hard boiled (hard-cooked) eggs, roughly cut up	*2*	*2*	*2*
Small onion, sliced and separated into rings	*1*	*1*	*1*
Tomatoes, diced	*4*	*4*	*4*
Can tuna in oil, drained reserving oil	*185 g*	*6¹/₂ oz*	*1 small can*
Can anchovies, drained and cut in thin slivers	*50 g*	*2 oz*	*1 small can*
Olive oil	*90 ml*	*6 tbsp*	*6 tbsp*
Red wine vinegar	*30 ml*	*2 tbsp*	*2 tbsp*
Salt and freshly ground black pepper			
To garnish			
Cos (romaine) lettuce leaves			
Chopped parsley			
A few black olives, stoned (pitted)			

1.   Cook the beans in boiling salted water for 5 minutes until just tender. Drain, rinse with cold water and drain again.

2.   Place in a bowl with the remaining ingredients and season lightly with salt and add lots of black pepper. Toss very gently so as not to break up the tuna too much.

Serving suggestion

Add to cooked conchiglie. Toss well but gently. Pile onto a bed
of lettuce leaves and garnish with chopped parsley and a few
black olives.

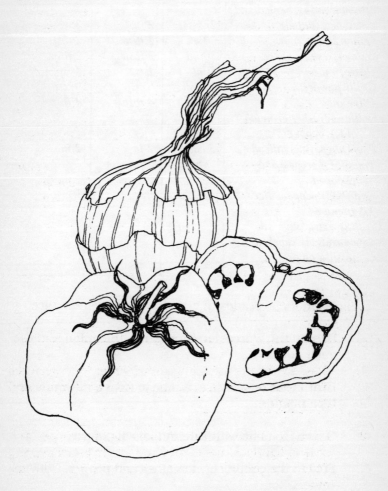 Preparation time: 15 minutes, including cooking the
beans

MEXICAN AVOCADO DRESSING

Guacamole is a popular dip for raw vegetables or tortilla chips. Try it as a sensational topping for pasta too!

Serves 4	Metric	Imperial	American
Ripe avocados, peeled and stoned (pitted)	2	2	2
Lemon juice	30 ml	2 tbsp	2 tbsp
Worcestershire sauce	30 ml	2 tbsp	2 tbsp
Grated onion	5 ml	1 tsp	1 tsp
Chilli powder	2.5 ml	$^1/_2$ tsp	$^1/_2$ tsp
Olive oil	60 ml	4 tbsp	4 tbsp
Salt and freshly ground black pepper			
Cucumber, finely diced	5 cm	2 in	2 in
Tomatoes, seeded and chopped	2	2	2
Red (bell) pepper, diced	$^1/_2$	$^1/_2$	$^1/_2$
To garnish			
A little extra olive oil			
A few roughly crushed tortilla chips			

1. Mash the avocados in a bowl with the lemon juice.

2. Beat in the Worcestershire sauce, the onion and the chilli powder.

3. Beat in the oil a little at a time to form a mayonnaise-type mixture.

4. Season to taste with salt and lots of pepper.

5. Fold in the cucumber, tomatoes and pepper. Chill for up to 1 hour.

Serving suggestion

Toss cold cooked tagliatelle verdi (green tagliatelle) in a little olive oil. Pile onto serving plates and top with the avocado mixture. Sprinkle with crushed tortilla chips just before serving.

 Preparation time: 10 minutes

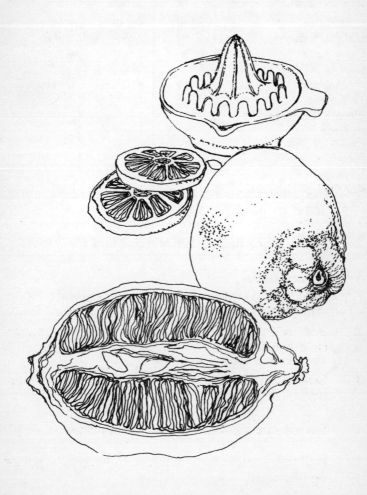

CURRIED CHICKEN MAYONNAISE

This is also delicious tossed into cold cooked rice. For more spice, increase the amount of curry paste used, or add a pinch of chilli powder.

Serves 4	Metric	Imperial	American
Mayonnaise	60 ml	4 tbsp	4 tbsp
Mango chutney	30 ml	2 tbsp	2 tbsp
Curry paste	10 ml	2 tsp	2 tsp
Cooked chicken, roughly chopped	175 g	6 oz	1½ cups
To garnish			
Mixed salad leaves			
Paprika			
Lemon wedges			

1. Blend the mayonnaise in a bowl with the mango chutney and curry paste.

2. Fold in the cooked chicken and chill until ready to serve.

Serving suggestion
Add to cold cooked wholewheat penne, toss well and pile onto a bed of mixed salad leaves. Garnish with paprika and lemon wedges before serving.

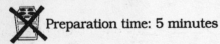 Preparation time: 5 minutes

PRAWN COCKTAIL SAUCE

Yes, this good old favourite is exquisite added to pasta for a main course – it makes the shellfish go further too!

Serves 4	Metric	Imperial	American
Mayonnaise	150 ml	1/4 pt	2/3 cup
Tomato ketchup (catsup)	15 ml	1 tbsp	1 tbsp
Single (light) cream	15 ml	1 tbsp	1 tbsp
Horseradish cream	10 ml	2 tsp	2 tsp
Stuffed olives, chopped	6	6	6
Hard-boiled (hard-cooked) egg, finely chopped	1	1	1
Green (bell) pepper, finely chopped	1/2	1/2	1/2
Peeled prawns (shrimp)	175 g	6 oz	1 1/2 cups
To garnish			
Shredded lettuce			
Snipped chives			
Twists of lemon			

1. Mix the mayonnaise with the tomato ketchup, cream and horseradish in a large bowl.

2. Add all the remaining ingredients and toss well but lightly. Chill until ready to serve.

Serving suggestion
Add to cold cooked farfalle. Toss gently but thoroughly. Pile onto a bed of shredded lettuce, sprinkle with snipped chives and garnish with twists of lemon.

 Preparation time: 8 minutes, plus chilling

WARM CRUNCHY FRIED BREAD AND HERB DRESSING

Use this dressing for either home-made or fresh bought pasta. Its simplicity is its elegance.

Serves 4	Metric	Imperial	American
Wholemeal breadcrumbs	225 g	8 oz	4 cups
Tomatoes, chopped	12	12	12
Sprigs of thyme, chopped	4	4	4
Chopped basil	45 ml	3 tbsp	3 tbsp
Chopped parsley	45 ml	3 tbsp	3 tbsp
Salt and freshly ground black pepper			
Olive oil	120 ml	4 fl oz	1/2 cup
Garlic cloves, crushed	3	3	3
To serve			
Freshly grated Parmesan cheese			

1. Dry-fry (sauté) the breadcrumbs in a large frying pan (skillet), tossing all the time until crisp but not brown.

2. Mix the tomatoes with the herbs, salt and lots of pepper.

3. Heat the oil in a frying pan, add the breadcrumbs and garlic and fry (sauté) until golden brown. Add to the bowl and toss well.

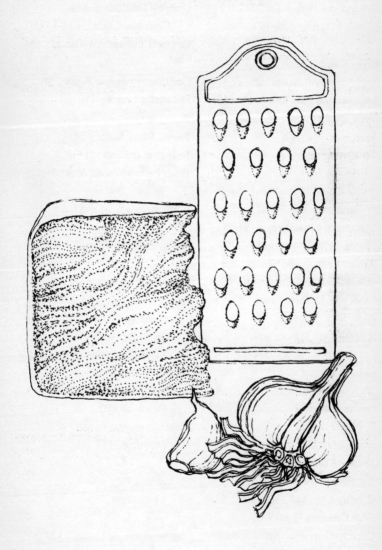

Index